5.95

DO YOU HEAR WHAT YOU'RE THINKING?

JERRY A. SCHMIDT

This book is designed for your personal reading pleasure and profit. It is also designed for group study. A Leader's Guide with helps and hints for teachers and visual aids (Victor Multiuse Transparency Masters) is available from your local bookstore or from the publisher.

D0181601

VICTOR BOOKS ®
A DIVISION OF SCRIPTURE PRESS PUBLICATIONS INC.
USA CANADA ENGLAND

Sixth printing, 1988

Unless otherwise indicated, Scripture quotations in this book are from the *New American Standard Bible* (NASB), © the Lockman Foundation 1960, 1962, 1963, 1968, 1971, 1972, 1973, 1975, 1977. Used by permission.

Recommended Dewey Decimal Classification: 171.1
Suggested Subject Heading: PSYCHOLOGY, BASED ON AUTHORITY

Library of Congress Catalog Card Number: 82-61036
ISBN: 0-88207-381-8

VICTOR BOOKS
A division of SP Publications, Inc.
Wheaton, Illinois 60187

Contents

Preface   5

1   Laying the Groundwork   7
2   Automatic Thinking   17
3   Countering: Arguing with Yourself   26
4   The Use of Imagery   37
5   The Use of Prayer and Meditation   45
6   Thinking Your Way Out of Depression   54
7   Stress and Anxious Thoughts   65
8   Guilt: Destructive and Not So Destructive   76
9   Speaking the Truth in Love   92
10   Perfectionism   112
11   Anger and Resentment   124
12   Self-Worth: The Bottom Line   134

Foreword

Every person carries on inner conversations. Often these conversations are referred to as self-talk. From our inner conversations come our feelings, reactions, perceptions, and even behaviors.

Is it possible to change self-talk? Is there a way to alter patterns of thinking which have been present for years? The answer is yes! Now there is a practical step-by-step guideline to make these changes a reality.

Jerry Schmidt has developed one of the most simple and practical approaches that I have ever read. Developed from his own research, teaching, and counseling experiences, the material presented in this volume has been tested and tried by many.

I highly recommend this book to all readers. Too often we are told what we need to do without the important step of how to do it. As you read you will discover the "how to" and will realize that changes can occur in your thinking styles and patterns.

H. Norman Wright

Director Christian MF
Faculty, Talbot Theological Seminary

Preface

What are you thinking? How often have you been asked that question? And how many times have you answered, "Oh, I don't know"? At this moment, you probably are not too aware of the thoughts that are actually affecting your behavior, your emotions, your life. You see, many of our thoughts are so automatic, so subconscious that we are not ever aware of them.

It's kind of like riding a bicycle. At first Dad might have said, "Turn the direction you're falling." And in the beginning you might have even verbalized these words audibly, or certainly thought about them as you struggled to keep upright on your two-wheeler. But after you had gained some expertise very little of your balancing was thought through consciously. Instead, you automatically and subconsciously thought, *Now turn this way, now that way*.

Most attitudes and behavior are learned in this way. Your responses to conflict, ways of showing love, your expressions of anger, are all motivated by subconscious self-talk. Some of these subliminal thoughts are constructive and helpful and positive behaviors result from them. But other subconscious self-talk motivates us to engage in self-destructive and other-destructive behavior.

How can all this be helpful? First, by discovering what undesirable thoughts are lurking beneath the surface. Second, by utilizing some promising methods for getting rid of these automatic beliefs. Third, by replacing these mental distortions with eternal truths. Through this three-step process you can help lift yourself out of depression. Perfectionism, destructive guilt, dehabilitating stress, and feelings of worthlessness can be dramatically decreased.

As a psychologist I have come to the conclusion that helping people change what they say to themselves is a key in giving them a new perspective. This book revolves around what we tell ourselves in the privacy of our own minds. Revealing these concealed conclusions to ourselves is the beginning of discovering truth that can be life-changing. But this process of puzzling over our conclusions about life is not easy. Redirecting trains of automatic thinking takes some mental exertion. It's hard work. Yet, time after time, I've seen the procedures described in the following pages bring about dramatic changes in people's lives.

1
Laying
the
Groundwork

"Men are not worried by things, but by their ideas about things. When we meet with difficulties, become anxious and troubled, let us not blame others, but rather ourselves; that is, our ideas about things" (Epictetus).

A major research project at Stanford University pointed to two critical variables in helping people change during the process of group psychotherapy. First, the group leader must be empathetic. The leader must be able to tune in to what others are saying. Second, and even more important, the group must serve the function of helping one another gain more constructive and meaningful philosophies of life. That is, the group that is successful will give its members better ways of thinking about their lives.

What do you think about? Scripture suggests that as a person "thinks within himself, so he is" (Prov. 23:7). H. Norman Wright, in a helpful book called *Improving Your Self-Image*, states:

"As we build up storehouses of memories, knowledge, and experiences we seem to retain and remember those things which we concentrate upon the most. If we concentrate upon rejection and hurt, they will be parts of our experience. Each person is responsible for the things he allows his mind to dwell upon."

The Apostle Paul told us what we are to think about: "Finally, brethren, whatever is true, whatever is honorable, whatever is right, whatever is pure, whatever is lovely, whatever is of good repute, if there is any excellence and if anything worthy of praise, let your mind dwell on these things" (Phil. 4:8). He also advised that we should set our minds and keep them set on what is above—the higher things—not on the things that are on the earth (Col. 3:2).

Herman Gockel writes, about your thought life:

"There is much more to this whole business than merely getting rid of negative or unworthy thoughts. In fact, the concept of 'getting rid' is itself a sign of negative thinking. The human mind can never be a vacuum. He who thinks he can improve the tenants of his soul simply by evicting those that are unworthy will find that for every unworthy tenant he evicts through the back door, several more will enter through the front. It is also a matter of screening, selecting, admitting, and cultivating those tenants that have proved themselves desirable."*

The principle of increasing positive things as opposed to decreasing negative things is basic to life.

Thought Patterns Can Be Changed

The Scripture promises that negative thinking can be changed to positive thinking: "Now your attitudes and thoughts must all be constantly changing for the better" (Eph. 4:23, LB). This is to be a continuing experience. As Paul wrote elsewhere, "Do not be conformed to this world, but be transformed by the renewing of your mind" (Rom. 12:2). The word "renewing" here means "making new from above." This implies that your thought-life can be renovated through prayer, searching God's Word, and believing in the working of the Holy Spirit.

In the background of Paul's writings is his conception of the Christian's growing likeness to Christ. Thus, in order to find

---

*Herman Gockel, *Answer to Anxiety*. St. Louis: Concordia, 1965, p. 156.

out the direction your thought-life ought to be moving, do an intensive study of Christ's life. Read the four Gospels: Matthew, Mark, Luke, and John. Use good Bible references such as Tyndale's or Barclay's New Testament commentaries. Based on your study, make a list of the kinds of thoughts that Christ probably had as He moved through His earthly life. These are the kinds of thoughts that we ought to be clinging to and constantly thinking.

We are, in fact, commanded by Paul to let our minds be filled with the mind of Christ. Paul directs us, "Let this mind be in you, which was also in Christ Jesus" (Phil. 2:5, KJV). The major point here is clear. We are to reflect in our own minds the mind of Jesus Christ. Whatever He thought about we too should be thinking about.

My mother-in-law, Myrtle Lambert, died of cancer a little over five years ago. During her struggle with this dread disease, she constantly turned to a particular Scripture passage which tells us what to stop thinking about and what to begin thinking about: "Do not fret or have any anxiety about anything, but in every circumstance and in everything by prayer and petition with thanksgiving continue to make your wants known to God. And God's peace, which transcends all understanding, shall garrison and mount guard over your hearts and minds in Christ Jesus. For the rest, brethren, whatever is true, whatever is worthy of reverence and is honorable and seemly, whatever is just, whatever is pure, whatever is lovely and lovable, whatever is kind and winsome and gracious, if there is any virtue and excellence, if there is anything worthy of praise, think on and weigh and take account of these things—fix your minds on them. Practice what you have learned and received and heard and seen in me. And model your way of living on it, and the God of peace—of untroubled, undisturbed well-being—will be with you" (Phil. 4:6-9, AMP).

Self-Talk
Debbie had hit rock bottom. She peered into her vanity mirror with a handful of aspirin, seeing nothing but the

reflection of an empty, lifeless face. For 10 years she had put up with beatings from a husband who did nothing else with her but use her sexually.

Bill always appeared to be such a wonderfully nice person to Debbie's parents, their church friends, and his work associates. No one but Debbie knew about the side of Bill that she called Mr. Hyde. She had tried desperately to make their relationship work, by serving Bill in every way. She mowed the lawn each week, trimmed the hedges, washed the cars, and kept them serviced. She never interrupted Bill when he was watching his favorite television show.

But the more she gave, the more Bill took, until he had nearly grasped the life out of her. Of course, Debbie had cooperated nicely in all of this. Her unconscious mind was playing "tapes," such as:

People must love me or I will be miserable.

If others criticize me, I must have done something wrong.

I must never show any weakness.

I should never hurt anyone.

Strong people don't ask for help.

With these kinds of beliefs buzzing in her head, how would you imagine that Debbie felt most of the time? She felt inferior, cautious, angry, resentful, and hurt.

But how do you suppose she behaved? She acted as if she were on top of the world. Debbie covered herself well under a smile and an "isn't God great?" attitude. If someone criticized her, she would become quiet and exit as soon as possible, yet graciously, so that no one would suspect she had any ill feelings. Certainly Deb never expressed anger or protested if someone came down on her. Furthermore, she would seldom confide in anyone or ask for any help from her friends.

At the moment she is contemplating taking her life. Debbie is full of anger. She is lonely, disillusioned, in complete despair. She has painted herself into a corner and it seems there is no way out.

Let's stop this downward spiral for a moment. Just suppose

that instead of some of the destructive "tapes," Debbie's mind were playing these:

I wish certain people would love me, but I can't make them do so!

If others criticize me, I may be wrong, but I need to check the facts and find out.

By showing my weaknesses to people I can trust, I'll have chances to get closer to others and to grow as a person.

Unfortunately, it is sometimes necessary to speak the truth in love, even if it occasionally hurts another person.

Strong people do ask for help. Even the Apostle Paul, when he was in prison, pleaded with Timothy to help him.

If Debbie were thinking in this way, how would she respond to her life's circumstances? She might become angry and express those feelings to a friend or directly toward her husband. She might confront her husband and tell him to either stop beating her or else! Debbie would be more likely to share her burdens with friends, asking them for help and receiving some badly needed support. She'd be far less likely to paint herself into a corner of loneliness and despair.

Do you see? What goes through our minds notably affects how we feel and what we do. There is physiological evidence which supports my view. This evidence states that the sensations and perceptions we receive or take in from the world around us are first absorbed and interpreted in the *thinking* centers of our brains. Next, we allow these same sensations to be transferred to our emotional centers. Thus we interpret and think about sensations *before* we develop feelings about them. It follows, then, that our thoughts dramatically affect our feelings and actions.

As Simple as ABC

The principles of this new therapy are as simple as ABC. A (the situation) doesn't cause C (our emotions and reactions); but rather B (our attitude or cognitive interpretation of A) triggers our emotions and reactions:

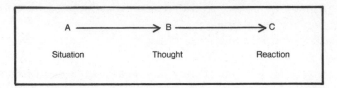

Let's illustrate this ABC theory with a practical example:

A. (SITUATION): Jeff couldn't start his car, so he was late for work.

B. (AUTOMATIC INTERPRETATION AND THOUGHTS): *Good employees aren't late for work. Everyone is disappointed and angry with me because I'm late.*

C. (RESULTING FEELINGS): Guilt, inferiority.

D. (RESULTING BEHAVIOR): Avoided people all day. Snapped at customers. Did not explain to boss why he was late.

At this moment you might be thinking, *What a self-defeating way to react. I'd never respond that way.* That's good! I hope you wouldn't. You see, at some level Jeff is really saying, "It's terrible to make mistakes." But that simply isn't so. What, then, would be a more healthy way to respond to this situation? Well, Jeff might have announced to his boss that his car had broken down and that he was sorry for being late. If Jeff had reacted in this way at C, what likely would have been his thinking at B? It might have gone something like this: *It's a real inconvenience for my car to break down just before work and I don't like it! I need to figure out what to do as rapidly as possible so I can get to work and explain what happened.*

Ready for another example?

A. (SITUATION): Alan Tentative was turned down for a date by Sally Upstart.

B. (AUTOMATIC INTERPRETATION AND THOUGHTS): *Women must think I'm undesirable. What's the use? I'm just plain worthless.*

C. (RESULTING FEELINGS): Inferiority, depression, embarrassment.

D. (RESULTING BEHAVIOR): Alan never called Sally again. In fact, he didn't call any other girl for over a month.

An overreaction you say? Certainly! But what caused Alan's response? Was it the situation (A)? No. It was Alan's interpretation (B again), that produced negative self-defeating results.

At this point you might be asking, "OK, but where do these negative Bs come from and how can I recognize them?" The answer is pretty straightforward. Most of these thoughts at B come from philosophies you've learned about life. They are picked up from parents, teachers, friends, movies, television. They can even be picked up at church. How can you recognize such self-defeating thoughts? By bringing them from the unconscious level to the conscious level. And how do you accomplish that? Chapters 2 and 3 will deal with the mechanics involved, but allow me to lay some more necessary groundwork before we get into nuts-and-bolts specifics.

Layer Theory

Lawrence J. Crabb, Jr., a noted Christian psychologist, has developed an interesting model for looking at human behavior.* He begins his model by asserting that human personality is structured in the following manner:

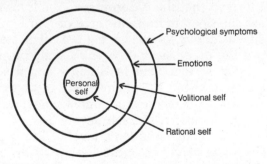

The most obvious manifestation of what is inside a person can be observed in his *psychological symptoms*. At this "layer," as he calls it, Dr. Crabb contends that we might see

---

*Lawrence J. Crabb, Jr., *Effective Biblical Counseling*. Grand Rapids: Zondervan, 1977.

symptoms of depression, for example. A person might be unable to sleep, lack any appetite, and avoid contact with others. These are typical outward signs or symptoms commonly seen in a person who is depressed.

At the next "layer" we can recognize *emotions* in a depressed person. Some of these emotions might include feelings of worthlessness, anger, guilt, and anxiety. Dr. Crabb contends that in order for a person to change in a positive direction, his symptoms and emotions must first be dealt with.

Then this same person needs to realize that he or she is a *volitional* being, who makes choices. For a depressed person, this would include looking at what he is *doing* to help promote his depression or happiness. What choices is he making?

At the next layer we have the *rational self,* where Bs are manufactured. But the Bs depend on how the very core of *personal self* is trying to work out its significance and security.

Let's develop this theory into practicality through illustrations. Let's say that a 35-year-old woman, Pam, is in my counseling office. As she shares with me I can see at the *symptomatic level* that she is depressed. She is losing weight. Rarely does she sleep more than three or four hours a night. Pam has suicidal thoughts and has cut herself off from friends. I've pierced the outer layer of Crabb's symptom level.

Next, I discover that Pam feels angry and frustrated because everyone else but she seems to be getting their needs met. She also feels some strong guilt whenever she doesn't measure up to standards she has set for herself. Thus, I'm beginning to pierce the *emotional* level of Pam's personality and thereby understand a bit more clearly what is causing her problems.

In order to cut through to Pam's *volitional* self I ask her what she does when she feels angry or guilty. Pam answers, "When I'm angry I don't tell anyone, but instead I become distant and withdrawn. When I feel guilty I apologize, probably too much, and I clobber myself internally." We then talk about the fact that she is, in part, making choices to behave in ways that keep her depressed. That is, if she continues to stuff her anger and withdraws from people, she will promote her depression. Often depression comes from anger that is turned inward.

Then I move into her *rational* area, asking her questions that help get at the Bs or self-defeating thoughts that are destroying her life. I find that some of her thoughts go like this:

I should feel guilty if I don't please others at all times.

I should never hurt anyone else's feelings.

I should never make mistakes. I must be perfect.

Can you see how such thoughts might cause Pam to feel frustrated, angry, and guilty?

Finally, I want to find out how Pam is attempting to work out her own *personal* worth. This is at the core of why Pam is depressed. Knowing this will help me form some positive strategies for hope. I find out that Pam was given a clear message as a little girl that she was worthwhile *if*:

She excelled.

She didn't make mistakes.

She did not *express anger.*

She expressed positive feelings only.

She was not *critical.*

So what do you think her goals in adult life became, in order to feel significant and secure? They are obvious. All we need to do is look back at what made her significant as a child and we have it. But are these realistic goals? Are they attainable? Are they worthwhile? Do they serve God's purposes? Do they follow biblical teachings?

What about the first goal? Pam was worthwhile *if* she excelled. How does this goal match up with the fact that Pam is a child of God, that she is accepted by Him as a less-than-perfect being? How does it match up with the concept of justification by faith? With God's unconditional love?

What about her second goal for worthiness? Pam is OK *if* she doesn't make mistakes. The Apostle Paul made mistakes, and he wrote over one-fourth of the New Testament! Was Paul worthwhile?

Jesus gave us the greatest commandment (Mark 12:28-31). We are to love God first, then ourselves. And if we do these two things, we will be free to love others. I don't read in Scripture that "You are worthwhile *if* and *only if* you do *not* make mistakes." Jesus came to deliver us into worthiness *because* we make mistakes, not to *condemn* us for our mistakes.

The point here is that the goals by which we try to work out our worthiness are critically important. They determine how we interpret situations and events. Suppose you say to yourself, *I will be significant if:*

> *I have money.*
> *I excel.*
> *I never make a mistake.*
> *I am a success.*
> *My kids turn out well.*
> *I am granted recognition by my peers.*
> *I am included in important circles.*

Then you are at the mercy of those goals for your worthiness. But if you say, "I *am* worthwhile *because* God created me in His image and because Christ died for me," then you're on a more realistic track. You are then less likely to reinforce goals and thoughts that can only lead to frustration, guilt, and anxiety.

One purpose of the ensuing chapters is to help you discover that your goals, and what you think and believe, largely determine how you feel and what you do. A second purpose of this book is to teach you *how* to change your fundamental, negative misbeliefs into more constructive, healthy ways of responding to life.

2
Automatic Thinking

Imagine you're single and out on a date with that special person. You are in a restaurant. Your date has been paying you undivided attention up to this point. Then all of a sudden he turns to the people at the next table and begins a conversation with them. What thoughts go through your mind? What does your self-talk sound like? Perhaps you think, *He must find me so boring that he can't continue talking with me. . . . He's ignoring me, deliberately!*

And what feelings would build up inside of you as you think these things? You would perhaps feel rejected, inferior, and angry. What sort of actions would likely follow? You might sulk, glare at him, become silent, or even leave the restaurant.

Such self-talk would likely be so spontaneous or automatic that when your date turned to talk with others, you might not be consciously aware of your thoughts. These automatic thoughts are somewhat unconscious or subconscious. The attitude or belief that others find you boring may have its roots deep in the past. It may be that you were the recipient of some pretty nasty peer rivalry as a child. Or perhaps you were deliberately ignored by your friends on several occasions, leaving you with some negative assumptions about your relationships with others. At first you may have consciously thought, *People find me boring; they're not interested in me*. But after repeatedly being disregarded by your friends, such conscious thoughts became automatic.

Now feelings of inferiority, rejection, and anger well up inside you every time someone pays you less attention than others. You no longer consciously remember the earlier experiences of being slighted. But, lurking in your subconscious mind, are the same assumptions: *People find me boring . . . I'm an unimportant, uninteresting person . . . most anyone would rather be with someone else*.

It's this kind of automatic thinking that must be uncovered if any change in behavior and feelings is to be accomplished. We said in chapter 1 that as a person "thinks in himself ('in his heart,' kjv), so he is" (Prov. 23:7). So we must first find out what it is that a person thinks "in his heart." Because what is in a person's heart determines who he is. The word "heart" means the center of a person's inward life. In the Old Testament, "heart" includes the emotions, the reason, and the will, three of the most crucial elements in a person. So, listen up! If you master the concept of automatic thoughts, half the battle is won.

Peter's Automatic Thoughts

Peter, Christ's disciple, was an interesting person. According to Maxie Dunnam, Peter was like a Marlboro man, a rugged individualist who thought he could make it on his own. But it was this same rugged guy who cowered like a defenseless kitten at the gaze of a woman who accused him of following Jesus. Why? Because he was embarrassed? Could be. But why was he embarrassed? Let's take another quick look at Larry Crabb's "layer theory," in chapter 1.

At the "symptom" layer Peter appeared defensive: "I don't even know this blankety-blank man."

Looking at the "emotional" layer Peter felt embarrassed, perhaps threatened.

His "volitional" self was choosing to behave like a tough,

independent man, yet in the expected, popular, "in" manner.

What was Peter doing in his "rational" layer? He might have been subconsciously thinking, *I'll feel embarrassed if I don't do the "in" thing—and being popular is the only way to feel significant. If I associate with a "loser," I'll be labeled as a loser.*

And finally, in the inner "personal" layer of his personality, how was Peter trying to work out his own personal worth? What goals was he shooting for in order to feel like a significant human being? We can only conjecture, of course. Yet, based on our analysis so far, perhaps Peter believed, *I will be significant if:*

I appear cool and tough.
I am granted recognition by my peers.
I am included in the group.
I associate with "winners."
I am not considered too religious and therefore a weak sissy.

And where did these beliefs come from? Perhaps from what his parents taught him. Maybe these attitudes were reinforced because when he acted on them, he felt significant. It could be that when Peter was cool and tough others saw him as a leader and a real he-man. So whenever Peter was able to reach his goal of coolness and toughness he felt worthwhile. And after repeated successes these attitudes and thoughts became automatic.

Hooray! So now we've tentatively figured out why Peter denied Christ. So what? So this: If you can figure out what self-defeating automatic thoughts are lurking beneath the surface of your consciousness, you can gain power over them. Satan loves to hear you speaking falsehoods and put-downs to yourself, especially if he can keep you unaware that you're even doing it! But God wants you to speak the truth to yourself.

Discovering Automatic Thoughts
Virginia, a woman I worked with in therapy, wished to improve her ability to express anger appropriately. A friend of

Virginia's had repeatedly shown up late for luncheons, meetings, tennis matches, and other mutual appointments. One afternoon, when her friend arrived an hour late for a luncheon at a fancy restaurant, Virginia stated directly, "Mary Ann, when you show up late for appointments I get angry and upset. Lately, I've felt pretty resentful and I'm afraid my resentment could end up hurting our relationship. I don't want that to happen. So, I'd really appreciate it if you'd arrive on time for our appointments."

Virginia had just used good communication skills in telling Mary Ann, assertively, how she felt and what she wanted. Mary Ann responded pretty favorably to the confrontation, apologizing and stating her intent to improve.

But suddenly Virginia felt embarrassed, ashamed, depressed, and fearful. She began to act sullen and noncommunicative during lunch. Then she remembered a strategy I had taught her in therapy. While Mary Ann went to the rest room Virginia grabbed a napkin and began writing down her thoughts, just whatever came to her mind. She began to scribble:

She probably thinks I'm a witch . . . She'll never speak to me again . . . I'm sure this will be our last lunch . . . probably our last anything . . . I'm sure she'll never call me again . . . There goes another friendship down the tube . . . It's a sin to express anger like that . . . God will punish me now for sure.

Later that evening as Virginia contemplated her sad experience she jotted down a few more automatic thoughts regarding her expression of anger. This helped clarify what was triggering her negative feelings.

Then she remembered the second part of the strategy I had taught her: "Ask yourself these questions: (1) Which of these automatic thoughts are true? Which thoughts follow Christian teachings? Why? Why not? (2) How do I know? (3) What are some alternative ways of thinking?

In looking at the thought, *She probably thinks I'm a witch*, Virginia realized that this assumption may or may not be true, and that one way for her to really know would be to ask Mary Ann. She decided to do so. Mary Ann reassured her and, in fact, stated she knew she had it coming and that Virginia's comment had made her aware of a real "blind spot." By calling Mary Ann, Virginia also checked out her second assumption, *She'll never speak to me again.* Mary Ann had, in fact, spoken to her again, and kindly at that!

In answer to my third question, "What are some alternative ways of thinking?" Virginia wrote:

I don't like being angry, but I'm not stuck with it. My thoughts and feelings are important. It's OK to confess them. The Bible says, "If you are angry, don't sin by nursing your grudge. Don't let the sun go down with you still angry—get over it quickly" (Eph. 4:26, LB). Being angry at someone doesn't have to lead to a loss of friendship. I've been angry toward friends before and we remained friends. Why not now also? Christ became angry from time to time, even with His disciples, but they still loved each other. I'll call her now and clear the air.

One way for you to discover your own automatic thoughts is to follow the same procedure Virginia did:

1. In a very tense situation write down all your automatic thoughts, whatever goes through your head about the situation.

2. As you look at your automatic thoughts *on paper*, ask yourself three questions:

    (a) Which of these automatic thoughts are true?

    (b) How do I know whether they are true or false?

    (c) What are some alternative ways of thinking?

3. *Write* answers to the last three questions.

4. *Save* this entire analysis and refer to it weekly to remind yourself of the truth.

Aaron T. Beck, an expert in the field of depression, has developed "The Daily Record of Dysfunctional Thoughts." His ideas may be used as a helpful adjunct to the strategies I had Virginia employ in her therapy. Following are two examples of the use of Beck's form.

A medical records librarian had a six-year history of depression:

Event	Feelings	Cognitions	Other possible interpretations
The charge nurse in the coronary unit was curt and said, "I hate medical records," when I went to collect charts for the record review committee.	Sadness, slight, anger, loneliness	She doesn't like me.	The charge nurse is generally unhappy. Hating medical records is not the same as hating me; she actually hates paperwork.
			She is under a lot of pressure for unknown reasons.
			She is foolish to hate records; they are her only defense in a lawsuit.

A 24-year-old nurse, recently discharged from a hospital for severe depression, presented this record:

Event	Feelings	Cognitions	Other possible interpretations
While at a party, shortly after I was discharged from the hospital, Jim asked me, "How are you feeling?"	Anxious	Jim thinks I am a basket case. I must really look bad for him to be concerned.	He really cares about me.
			He noticed that I look better than before I went into the hospital and wants to know if I feel better too.*

Charts such as the above may be used as permanent reminders of the kinds of situations and errors in thinking that have maintained or have accentuated your own difficulties.

---

*A. Beck, J. J. Rush, B. F. Shaw, G. Emery, *Cognitive Therapy of Depression*. New York: The Guilford Press, 1979.

Look At the Past

Another method for discovering automatic thoughts that are plaguing you now is to examine your past. Here's how. Again, do this in the form of a written exercise.

1. Describe your mother and father separately. What were they like when you were little (8-10 years of age)? How did they feel? Based on their behavior and their feelings, what likely were some of *their* automatic thoughts?

2. Close your eyes, and one at a time imagine the face of each of your parents staring into your eyes. What does each parent say to you, *nonverbally*, by the expressions on his and her face? What does each face say to you *verbally?* Are there any "shoulds," or "should-nots"?

3. Jot down 10 recollections from your childhood, before age 8 or 9 if possible. Make them *specific* events, not general. Next to each experience write what you were probably feeling and thinking at the time. What did you learn from each recollection? Any automatic thoughts that you may have carried through to today?

Want another method of pinpointing your automatic thoughts? Look at the following list developed by Rian McMullin and Bill Casey. If a thought strikes home, jot it down and submit that thought to the same analysis that my patient Virginia did.

Thoughts that Cause Problems

1. People must love me or I will be miserable.
2. Making mistakes is terrible.
3. People should be condemned for their wrongdoing.
4. It is terrible when things go wrong.
5. My emotions can't be controlled.
6. I should be terribly worried about threatening situations.
7. Self-discipline is too hard to achieve.
8. I *must* depend on others.
9. My childhood must always affect me.
10. I can't stand the way others act.

11. Every problem has a perfect solution.
12. I should be better than others.
13. If others criticize me, I must have done something wrong.
14. I can't change what I think.
15. I should help everyone who needs it.
16. I must never show any weakness.
17. Healthy people don't get upset.
18. There is only one true love.
19. I should never hurt anyone.
20. There is a magic cure for my problems.
21. It's others' responsibility to solve my problems.
22. Strong people don't ask for help.
23. I can do things only when I'm in the mood.
24. Possible is the same as probable.
25. I am inferior.
26. I am always in the spotlight.
27. People ought to do what I wish.
28. Giving up is always the best policy.
29. I need to be sure before I decide.
30. Others should always be sure before they decide.
31. Change is unnatural.
32. Knowing how my problems started when I was young is essential.
33. Everybody should trust me.
34. I should be happy all the time.
35. There is a secret, terrible part of me that controls me.
36. Working on my problems could hurt me.
37. The world ought to be fair.
38. I am not responsible for my behavior.
39. It is always better not to be genuine.
40. I have no problems.
41. Anxiety is always dangerous.
42. You can't tell me anything about myself that I don't know.
43. People shouldn't act the way they do.

44. I should be able to control my kids' (or spouse's) behavior.
45. Willpower alone can solve all my problems.*

Finally, keep in mind, we are building skills. This chapter on "Automatic Thinking" is a prerequisite for the next chapter. Thus, it does *not* contain all the strategies you will learn. Be patient. I do not wish to overwhelm you all at once with too many strategies. Work on automatic thinking first, and become thoroughly familiar with it. For it forms the basis of all that follows.

---

*R. McMullin and B. Casey, *Talk Sense to Yourself*. Lakewood, Colorado: Creative Designs, 1975.

3
Countering: Arguing with Yourself

Once you discover your automatic thoughts which are self-destructive and not in line with biblical teaching, you can begin to challenge them. The way most people get rid of irrational thoughts is by arguing with them. That is, we fight irrational thoughts with reason. It's something most people do so naturally that they don't even know they are doing it. In a scary movie, for instance, we may tell ourselves, *It's only a movie.* When a child acts rudely, we may remind ourselves, *He just isn't old enough to know any better.* When a foreigner behaves in a way that we find strange, we may say to ourselves, *Of course he acts differently; he's from a different culture.* All of these thoughts tend to calm us down a little. Realistic thoughts such as these can be automatic, just as self-defeating thoughts can be.

Such realistic thoughts, which are more in line with the actual truth of the matter than our self-defeating thoughts, are called *counters.* The process of stopping an irrational thought is called *countering.* Countering replaces the negative thinking which leads you to feel and respond negatively. Here are some examples of irrational thoughts and their counters:

IRRATIONAL THOUGHT: *I have nothing to offer.*

26

COUNTER: *That's ridiculous.*

COUNTER: *Several friends enjoy my company. They've told me so!*

COUNTER: *There's no way that thought can help me!*

IRRATIONAL THOUGHT: *I must never show any weakness.*

COUNTER: *Says who?*

COUNTER: *That's simply not consistent with biblical teaching!*

COUNTER: *Even Christ showed "weakness" when He wept or when He asked His friends to watch and pray with Him at Gethsemane.*

IRRATIONAL THOUGHT: *I should be happy all the time.*

COUNTER: *Now that's a real impossibility!*

COUNTER: *Who needs that thought? It just places tremendous pressure on me!*

COUNTER: *If I were happy all the time, I'd be denying lots of feelings.*

Deciding If an Automatic Thought Is Irrational

Not all automatic thoughts are irrational. If they were we'd be in constant turmoil. In fact, hopefully, most of your automatic thoughts are realistic and helpful. You've learned lots of good philosophies and teachings from significant adults and peers in your past, and you will continue to. So, just because you begin to write down your automatic thoughts, even during a crisis, this does not necessarily mean that all of your thoughts are untrue. So how do you decide? One way is to submit your thoughts to the questions I listed in chapter 2:

1. Which of these automatic thoughts are true? Which thoughts follow Christian teachings? Why? Why not?

2. How do I know whether they are true or false?

3. What are some alternative ways of thinking?

Putting Your Thoughts on Trial

A second way to determine whether your automatic thoughts are true is to put them on trial. During this process you look for evidence that supports and refutes what's going through your mind. There's no point in gathering evidence, however, unless it is relevant to your problem. For example, if you wanted to know whether the population of Vermont was over 365,000 what would be the best kind of evidence? It would probably be ridiculous to go around asking what most people thought was the population of Vermont and then accept the average of the stated answers. Instead you would probably want to look in an almanac or check out some other source of authority.

Rian McMullin and Bill Casey have identified five methods to prove or disprove an automatic thought. They are:

1. Use your senses (seeing, hearing, tasting, touching, smelling).
2. Ask an authority.
3. Find out what most people think.
4. Use your own reasoning and logic.
5. Use your own experience.*

Let's see how some of these five methods can be used to determine the legitimacy of your automatic thoughts and help challenge your negative self-talk.

AUTOMATIC THOUGHT (spoken by a person who couldn't start his car in the morning): *I'm just plain stupid.* In order to put this thought on trial you might *use your own reasoning and logic* by asking yourself some of the following questions:
What rational basis do I have for telling myself that I'm stupid? I can usually figure things out. How would I define stupid? To me, stupid means "dumb in every way." How can one event in which I don't know something or can't figure out something make me draw the conclusion that I'm "dumb in every way"?

You might also *find out what most people think* by asking these questions:
Where is the evidence that people think I am a complete idiot? Can I

---

*R. McMullin and B. Casey, *Talk Sense to Yourself.* Lakewood, Colorado: Creative Designs, 1975.

read others' minds and know what they are thinking? Who has ever told me that I'm just plain stupid? What, in fact, do people say regarding my intelligence? Don't people think I'm simply another fallible human being like everyone else?

Or you could *use your own experience* by asking and answering: *What does my experience tell me about whether I'm an idiot or not? I succeeded in learning how to enclose my patio last year. I graduated from high school, and I passed several college courses. This proves that I'm not stupid about some things and that I can learn about things I'm unfamiliar with.*

Finally, you could *ask an authority:*

What have my teachers told me about my abilities? My professors? What kind of report did my boss turn in on me? She said I was one of her better employees in terms of getting the job done and doing it right. And even if my supervisor's evaluation had been negative that, in itself, would not prove that I'm "plain stupid." Who says I should be able to do everything right the first time I try? What does the ultimate authority, Scripture, have to say about my being stupid?

Let's look at another example and again utilize some of our methods for examining evidence.

NEGATIVE THOUGHT (by employee who is criticized by boss): *My boss is a horrible person. I am always being criticized and insulted by him. He makes me angry every day.*

Use your reasoning and logic: What rational basis do I have for telling myself that my boss is a horrible person? Isn't he just a fallible human being who does things I don't like? Doesn't practically everyone do things that someone doesn't like?

Use your own experience: Am I always being criticized and insulted? To say that I am always being insulted means that every second I am being met with critical remarks. That's silly. My experience tells me that only occasionally are critical remarks directed toward me.

Countering

Putting your thoughts on trial and examining the evidence leads to a process called countering. When you "counter" an irrational, self-defeating thought you fight it with your reason. By asking some of the questions in the previous section you will discover counters that you can use on a daily basis to counteract your irrational thoughts. Here are some other examples of irrational thoughts and their counters:

IRRATIONAL THOUGHT: *Since my boss criticized me that means I'm no good.*

COUNTER (finding out what most people think): *My boss criticizes everybody!*

COUNTER (using my experience): *That's the first time he's criticized me in over a week.*

IRRATIONAL THOUGHT: *She looks like a very interesting person, but she probably wouldn't be interested in me.*

COUNTER (using my experience): *How do I know? I haven't asked her!*

COUNTER (using logic): *What can I lose by trying to meet her?*

IRRATIONAL THOUGHT: *I'd better not disagree with what they are saying, because then they might not like me.*

COUNTER: *If they don't know what I think they'll never have a chance to decide whether or not they like me.*

COUNTER: *That puts me in a horrible position, where I can only agree!*

IRRATIONAL THOUGHT: *Healthy people don't get anxious or upset.*

COUNTER: *In my view, Dwight Eisenhower was a healthy person, and he certainly got upset and anxious at times.*

COUNTER: *The Gospels certainly describe Jesus as feeling anxious and upset from time to time. If He wasn't healthy, who was?*

Counters should be statements of reality. In other words, if your irrational thought is, *I am inferior in every way,* a poor counter would be, *No I'm not, I'm superior in every way.* A good counter will usually come from one of the five methods described earlier for putting your thoughts on trial. A realistic counter might come from simply asking other people for feedback about your ability. From this process you might come up with a counter such as, "Everyone I asked stated that I was good at several things."

Counters should be personally believable. A counter might include anything from a Scripture passage to a simple *Baloney!* The important point is that you really "buy into" the counters you use. For example, don't just pick a Bible verse because someone else in authority says it's the right one. Find one that speaks directly to you, both personally and emotionally.

Countering can either be done during a difficult situation or as part of what we'll call a rehearsal exercise. First let's talk about the use of a counter in a real-life situation. You are about to call an old friend. You give yourself some irrational thoughts such as, *I'd like to call my friend, but since she hasn't called me by now, she probably doesn't want to talk to me*. Then you remind yourself to counter and begin to actively think to yourself. *That's ridiculous! If I want to talk to her, it's my responsibility to call her!* The result is that you call your friend, she is delighted that you did, and you end up setting a luncheon date.

The counters that you use on the spot should be as active and persuasive as possible. Shout them out in your head! Scream internally at your self-defeating thoughts! Use several arguments against each irrational thought.

All the counters used in this chapter are arguments with thoughts, not emotions. That's why a counter such as, *No, I'm not sad*, is a poor one. That kind of argument only hides feelings and is potentially harmful. A better counter for "sadness" would be to attack the self-defeating thoughts which are leading you to escalate your sadness and make the situation worse than is warranted. Perhaps something like this would be better: *I'm sad because I failed to get the job I applied for, but this does not mean that I will never find work. I have other alternatives to interview tomorrow*. Argue against the thought, not the feeling.

Let's take another on-the-spot countering example. You haven't taken any vacation for quite a spell. You feel the doldrums setting in and you want to ask for some time off. Yet some irrational thoughts are holding you back: *If I ask for vacation time, my boss will probably think I'm a lazy good-for-nothing and I'll blow my chances for a raise.* At that point you begin to counter aggressively and realistically: *I've never seen him respond that way to anyone. Besides, I'm just mind reading. I do not have information that supports this self-defeating thought. Furthermore, vacation time is my right. I've earned it. I need it for myself and for my family.*

If you have difficulty coming up with good, sound arguments against irrational thoughts, here are two things you might try. One, think of someone you know who handles troublesome situations well. What does he probably say to himself that triggers him to act appropriately in such situations? How would that person argue with you, if you told him or her your irrational thought? Two, go ahead and actually ask that person for some counters or arguments.

Countering Practice

Peter tells us, "Gird your minds for action" (1 Peter 1:13). The words refer to "mental exertion." Peter implies an active, aggressive approach to filling our minds with positive, fulfilling thoughts. It's hard work to retrain our heads to say more constructive things than we've been used to. And it takes practice! Here are four more situations with their accompanying negative self-thoughts which result in self-defeating feelings and behaviors. A few counters for each negative thought are included. Add some counters of your own for practice.

SITUATION: Belinda is unhappy because someone she is very close to is moving to another city.

NEGATIVE THOUGHT: *I should be happy all the time. Christians should not be unhappy.*

RESULTING FEELINGS: Unworthiness, shame.

RESULTING BEHAVIOR: Belinda does not express to her friend

that she will miss her. Her friend gets the picture that Belinda doesn't care that she's leaving.

COUNTERS (arguments against the negative thought):

1. *That's nonsense! I can't think of one biblical character who was happy all the time.*

2. *That thought is a great way to lose friends fast!*

3. *That's dumb! I'm trying to be God.*

4. *Whoever told me that? Certainly my pastor has never suggested it!*

5. *(You add one)* _____

6. *(Another)* _____

SITUATION: Mike is sitting alone in his apartment. Several things have gone wrong for him this week and he'd like to be able to get some support from someone, but he hesitates.

NEGATIVE THOUGHT: *Strong people don't ever ask for help.*

RESULTING FEELINGS: Extreme loneliness, dejection

RESULTING BEHAVIOR: Mike stays in his apartment all weekend. He even gets drunk.

COUNTERS:

1. *Moses asked for help from God continually. He asked God for help to be able to speak to the Israelites. And Moses became one of the greatest leaders Israel ever had.*

2. *Other people I know ask for help continually.*

3. *I often help other people with their problems. Aren't I entitled to the same?*

4. *It's OK not to be perfect.*

5. *This thought only hurts me.*

6. *(Your turn!)* _____

7. *(Again)* _____

SITUATION: Sally Harried feels that she needs some time just for herself, away from her children. Yet she does nothing to make this happen.

NEGATIVE THOUGHT: *My children and my husband will think I'm terribly selfish if I ask to have some time to be left alone.*

RESULTING FEELINGS: Resentment, depressed resignation

RESULTING BEHAVIOR: Sally remains at home, becomes more upset with her children, begins shouting at them more frequently. One day she beats one of them leaving bruises.

COUNTERS:

1. *I have a right to some time alone.*

2. *Having some time away from the children will help me come back to them refreshed at the end of the day.*

3. *I have no reason to believe that they will think I'm selfish.*

4. *The Gospels report several instances when Jesus needed to be alone. He's my example.*

5. _____

6. _____

SITUATION: Ellen's daughter wants to borrow the car whenever she pleases.

NEGATIVE THOUGHT: *My daughter will probably hate me if I don't let her use the car whenever she wants to.*

RESULTING FEELING: Scared

RESULTING BEHAVIOR: Ellen lets her daughter take the car whenever she pleases.

COUNTERS:

1. *I have a right to say no. It's my car.*

2. *She will not respect me as a parent unless I stand up for what I believe in.*

3. *This thought will lead me to act in ways that I don't want!*

4. *In the long run, this kind of thinking will only hurt my relationship with her.*

5. *Disagreeing with someone does not always lead to quarreling and fights.*

6. _____

7. _____

The Note Card Technique

One of the simplest, most effective strategies for putting counters to good use is the note card technique. On one side of a 3" × 5" note card write down your automatic, irrational thought. On the same side, after the thought, print the words STOP! GO AWAY! or QUIT BUGGING ME! in capital letters. On the flip side of the card, write out some counters. Utilize "putting your thoughts on trial" and other strategies mentioned previously to develop good strong counters. Use God's Word.

Keep the card with you at all times. Whenever you begin to experience negative feelings related to your irrational thought, pull out the card. Read the irrational thought and the word STOP directly beneath it. Say it aggressively. If you are alone, say it out loud. If you're with people, scream it internally: *STOP!* Then turn the card over and read those beautiful, powerful counters. Relish each word as you read it. If you've included Scripture, meditate for a while on the verses. Let the truth of these words really sink in! The effect this will have is to first punish or break the chain of automatic negative thinking by giving yourself the cue to STOP. Then you will replace the irrational thoughts with some alternative thinking about the *truth*.

I've been excited by the positive results of this technique in counseling. After a few weeks people begin to memorize counters and Scriptures that automatically come to mind in stressful situations. But it takes work and repetition. Memorizing Scripture in this way is an excellent strategy for filling your mind with the truth that comes from above. It's an uplifting experience to hear a passage from God's Word piercing into your awareness in the midst of turmoil. Try it!

Read through your counters several times or until you begin to feel better internally. Post some of your counters in front of you, perhaps on your desk at work. Tape other counters with accompanying Bible verses on your refrigerator door, bedroom mirror, or on the dash of your car. Place these helpful statements wherever you will be sure to see them frequently.

One person I know has recorded his own voice reading counters and portions of Scripture that he finds helpful in warding off worry. He spends his devotional time driving to work in the morning, listening to these calming statements on his tape deck. It has helped him cope with his own fears much more effectively.

In subsequent chapters I'll list specific, typical irrational thoughts, counters, and Scriptures that correspond with each problem area. Now! Arise! Go Forth! And Counter!

4
The
Use of
Imagery

Susan picked up a cup of coffee. She was shaking so badly that she spilled some on the Donaldsons' new carpet. Her hand felt as though it had been scalded. Embarrassment welled up inside her. Suddenly her embarrassment turned to anger. *How stupid can you get, Sue?* she thought. *You're a nervous wreck, you idiot! Why is God putting me through all this hell? Doesn't He give a rip about me?*

Throughout the rest of the evening Susan tormented herself with thoughts such as, *I'll never make it. I might as well give up! No one at this party likes me anyway. They all think I'm inadequate. I am inadequate. I don't have one interesting thing to say to anyone. The only reason that I was even invited is because everyone likes Chad, my husband. So they figured they'd better let me tag along!*

As the party continued, Susan became more and more anxious, sullen, and quiet. Finally, she got Chad off in a corner and demanded that they go home early. Sobbing all the way home in the car, Susan began to scream, "How can you put up with me? I don't deserve you, Chad! Just divorce me and get it over with!"

At this point, Chad blew up. "What are you getting so messed up about, Susan? I'm sick and tired of us leaving parties early, and not going anywhere!"

When we started therapy, Susan related several incidents to me, all similar to the one just given. I told her to record her automatic thinking, list alternative thoughts, and to use note cards for countering. These tactics were helpful, but they did not move Susan along as rapidly as I had hoped. So I suggested some imagery methods.

Cognitive Rehearsal

Rehearsal is important in developing new skills. My nine-year-old son, Cory, and I have taken piano lessons. We both know the value of practicing our songs before a lesson. Directors of plays realize the importance of rehearsals before the actual performance.

One good way of "practicing" for the actual performance of any act is to rehearse it beforehand in your imagination. I'm sure you have done this many times, perhaps without realizing it. For example, when you are asked to give a short talk you may run it through in your mind several times, to organize your thoughts and words. You might imagine people asking you different questions and how you would like to answer them.

Or perhaps you've decided to bring up a touchy issue with a friend. In order to prepare yourself for the potential conflict, you might have rehearsed in your imagination exactly how to state your case. And you probably also imagined possible retorts from your friend and how you would handle them. These "cognitive rehearsals" can be powerful helps when the real situations arise.

A recent research study illustrates my point. Some scientists selected three groups at random to shoot basketballs from the free throw line. All groups were approximately equal in basketball-shooting ability. Soon, the first group was allowed to go home. The second group was given hours of practice shooting free throws. The third group was given the same amount of time to *just think about* making free throws successfully. They imagined themselves performing all the correct movements involved in shooting a basketball.

What do you think the results were? The first group, that was sent home, did not improve their basket-sinking ability. The second group, which had actual practice, improved significantly. And the third group, that merely thought about shooting free throws correctly, also improved significantly! In fact, they improved roughly as much as those who had hours of practice!

Voluntary Cortical Inhibition

After having given Susan roughly the same groundwork I've just given you on "cognitive rehearsal," I suggested the Voluntary Cortical Inhibition strategy or VCI for short. Cortical has to do with the cortex or the intellect, the memory thought processes and rational centers of the brain. Therefore, VCI or Voluntary Cortical Inhibition, merely means to voluntarily inhibit certain thoughts. How is this done?

1. CREATE A HIERARCHY LIST. You develop a hierarchy or situations which produce a single emotion, such as *anger, guilt, anxiety, shame*, or *depression*. These situations may have actually happened to you or they could be something that you imagine might happen. You should write these situations on separate index cards (one situation per card), and then rank them from 1 to 10 in terms of their severity. For example, if we were creating a hierarchy of *anxiety* for Susan, we would first write *anxiety* items on 10 cards and then rank each card on a scale of 1 to 10. Ten produces the most anxiety and 1 the least.

It's important that you rank the anxiety level of each card evenly so that the situation ranked at 2 would produce only slightly more anxiety than the situation which you ranked at 1. When you finish the first step you should have 10 situations, evenly ranked from 1 to 10.

Here is Susan's hierarchy on *anxiety*. Remember, this is only her list. Your own items and their arrangement might be much different.

1. Watching someone else give a speech.

2. Contemplating going to a party that's coming up in a week.

3. Sitting in church next to someone I don't know well.

4. Sitting in a night class listening to a lecture, knowing I may be called on to answer a question.

5. Going out with another couple we know fairly well.

6. Sitting in a Sunday School class at church where discussion is encouraged.

7. Being called on to pray in our Koinonia sharing group.

8. Meeting a stranger, getting to know him for the first time.

9. Seeing my children misbehave in public.

10. Trying to make conversation with acquaintances and strangers at a social gathering of several people.

2. DEVELOP A LIST OF COUNTERS. Once you have created your hierarchy, develop a list of counters. Remember how to do that? If not, review chapter 3. If your hierarchy, like Susan's, is based on *anxiety,* you should develop some standard counters for *anxiety* feelings. Susan, for example, created the following counters: *What good do all these put-downs do me? Putting myself down really helps nothing! God says to be anxious for nothing!* (Phil. 4:6) *Instead of concentrating so heavily on myself, I'll concentrate on someone else. I'm "catastrophizing" again! Nobody's perfect! What am I doing to myself?*

3. APPLY VOLUNTARY CORTICAL INHIBITION PRINCIPLES. Using your list of counters, do the following:

A. Imagine the lowest item on your hierarchy. Think of this item as vividly and clearly as possible by using all your senses to imagine it. Then, envision saying self-defeating thoughts to yourself.

B. Internally shout, *STOP!* to yourself. Or scream internally, *Get away from me, idiot thought!* Or, *Quit bugging me!* Or, *What a stupid thought!* (What you are doing here is inhibiting or punishing your self-defeating thoughts.) Then immediately begin to counter as aggressively as you can. Really go after your irrational thinking (*not after yourself*).

Mentally shout your best counters. Some people even say them out loud. Attack those unrealistic assumptions. Contradict them! Use the counters you've developed in Step 2. Challenge the self-defeating thoughts as hard as you can. Do this for about 30 seconds.

C. Repeat the above VCI procedure until you are no longer bothered by that situation.

D. Go directly to the next item on your hierarchy list, using the same procedure, until none of the situations on your hierarchy list bother you anymore.

Here is an example of a VCI for a person who is working on *fear*:

A. She starts working on the lowest item on her hierarchy list, "Son is playing football." She imagines the scene in full detail: *I go to the Saturday morning football game. My son is playing on the defensive team. A larger boy from the opposing team carries the ball. My son tries to tackle him and gets stepped on and falls to the ground. He is slow in getting up. I say to myself,* Ryan is probably hurt much worse than he's showing. He's probably got something serious that will show up in later life. He's bound to get hurt seriously. It's just a matter of time. *I begin to feel very fearful.*

B. She immediately shouts to herself, STOP! Then she counters hard and fast: *No one on the team has been hurt seriously for the past two seasons. Why would Ryan be singled out. He* did *get back up again! Ryan could get hurt seriously doing any number of things, but he hasn't. Besides, what good does it do him or me to be this fearful? Will my fearfulness change anything?*

Self-Punishment/Self-Reward

The SP/SR exercise is one of the most helpful imagery techniques for working on more realistic thinking. It is similar to VCI in that you are again using your imagination plus strong, aggressive, active thinking. To start using the Self-Punishment/Self-Reward technique you first relax, close your eyes, and let yourself unwind for a few moments. Let your hands

and arms grow warm and heavy . . . your shoulders . . . chest
. . . stomach . . . and legs. Let yourself get very heavy.
Remember, this is your time to relax and to work on your
head. When you feel relaxed, follow these directions:

1. Imagine the lowest item on your hierarchy. Once again,
picture and experience that scene very clearly. "See" the colors
and shapes; "hear" the sounds; notice the details in your imagined scene. Next, picture yourself stating a few of your self-
defeating thoughts. Actually allow yourself to feel the negative
emotion you are working on. When you feel it, STOP.

2. Immediately start imagining the worst possible consequences of your unhelpful thoughts. Let your imagination run
wild. For example, *If I keep thinking that making mistakes is
terrible, I'll watch my every move. If I get that uptight I'm
likely to become even* more *anxious and will increase my
chances for* making *mistakes!* Just let your thoughts run wild
with regard to the possible aversive consequences of irrational thinking. Do this for about 30 seconds; then stop.

3. Again, think of your same hierarchy item. Again, visualize it in great detail. However, this time imagine yourself
making more rational statements. Picture yourself handling
the situation beautifully, feeling good, acting calmly and ra-
tionally. Once you have performed this sequence (situation,
rational thoughts, positive reaction), stop.

4. Begin, at once, imagining the best possible consequences of your positive thoughts and reactions. Use your
creativity and feel free to exaggerate. For example, *If I can
realize that making mistakes is not awful, that it only shows
I'm human, I'll begin to take a few more risks. I'll begin to
trust God more. If I learn to trust Him more I'll probably be a
lot more at ease about life. I won't be so uptight and careful
about everything I say and do. I'll be much more fun to be
around, and others will respond to me more favorably* . . .
Keep on doing this for about 30 seconds.

Repeat this entire procedure until you feel at ease with the
particular scene you are imagining. Then work up your hierarchy list to scene 2 and work on it until you feel relatively

calm and confident. Then do scene 3 and so on.

Here's an example of an SP/SR for someone working on *anger:*

1. He clearly pictures the lowest item on his hierarchy. *I come home from work. My son, Brett, had promised to mow the lawn this morning, but hasn't touched it. In fact, Brett is gone playing at a friend's house. I ask my wife why she hasn't reinforced my decision and she tells me that neither Brett nor she could get the mower started. So he gave up and went over to Paul's house. I begin to think, "That kid is never responsible. He has an excuse for everything! He is completely irresponsible!" I start throwing things.*

2. He imagines the worst possible consequences of his self-defeating thoughts: *If I really believe that when things do not go my way it's terrible, I'll continue to throw tantrums whenever people don't do what I want them to. The more I explode, the less people will respect me. Then things will go even less my way because my children will likely start rebelling or will resist me passively. As they resist more strongly, I'll react with more anger. What a vicious cycle! All this anger will even affect my marriage!*

3. He again pictures the same scene in his mind. But this time he reacts with rational thoughts: *I come home from work. My son, Brett, had promised to mow the lawn this morning, but hasn't touched it. In fact, Brett is gone playing at a friend's house. I ask my wife why she hasn't reinforced my decision and she tells me that neither Brett nor she could get the mower started. So he gave up and went over to Paul's house. I begin to think, "Brett usually mows the lawn. I'll show him how to troubleshoot the mower. I can see why Brett decided to give up. Sometimes that mower is tough to start."*

4. Then he began imagining the best consequences of his positive thoughts and reactions: *If I truly believe that it's not so terrible when things don't go my way, then I'll be less apt to provoke my children to wrath, my children will more likely respect me, my wife will see the results of my more reasonable thinking and respect me more. If these things happen, my*

children will more than likely respond affirmatively to my requests. Then I will feel better about myself. I'll also know that I am pursuing God's purposes and not merely my own desires. Doing that will make me truly significant.

Some Final Thoughts about Your Imagination

We return to Proverbs 23:7: "As [a man] thinketh in his heart, so is he" (KJV).

James (4:7-8) concludes that we are to *submit* our thoughts to God and *resist* thoughts that are from the devil. In the Greek, *submit* means to "put oneself under, to be subject to." Another definition is "to obey." In our imaginations, then, we are to picture ourselves in complete obedience toward God. We are to plan in our minds to serve God's purposes. The Greek word translated *resist* means "to set against" or "to range in battle against." Those are fighting words!

Remember in our first chapter how we reach true significance? Real significance comes from serving God's purposes. How do we serve God's purposes? By *submitting* our thoughts and imaginations to God and *resisting* thoughts and imagery that are evil. How do we decide which part of our imagination is of God and which part is evil? By studying God's Word and determining how Christ and such people as Paul, Peter, Timothy, and others ran their lives. Picture their lives in your imagination. See yourself moving through life the way they did, *thinking* the way they did! What thoughts would you guess they reflected on? What pictures did they envision? What did they rehearse in their own imaginations? What did they plan to do in their premeditations? What trains of thought did these great Christian leaders have to resist? How did they resist? What did Timothy meditate on and ponder in order to behave in a manner "above reproach," as Paul put it? (1 Tim. 3—5)

Spend some time researching Scripture, and writing answers to the above questions. What you imagine, think on, contemplate, ponder, study, and glue your attention to *will* determine in a large part who you become.

5
The Use of Prayer and Meditation

There were scars, many scars, in Jennifer's past. Her father would often arrive home drunk, ready for a fight. And he would get it. Mom would be ready for him. She'd say, "Drunk again, huh? There goes our grocery money for the week, you pig!"

The battles that would follow were usually both verbal and physical. Mom would end up with blood on her somewhere and Dad would throw objects around the room. Perhaps the saddest were the times when Jennifer would try to break up the battles. In panic, she would often throw herself between Mom and Dad to keep them from hurting each other. Of course, the result was often harmful. Jennifer would walk away with a bloody nose, bruises, and once a broken arm. With that kind of past, you might imagine her inner pain.

And her inner pain was affecting her present functioning as a young woman. Jennifer mistrusted men. She was frightened of them. She was also angry with men. But at the same time she had a desire for a relationship with a male. Her fear, mistrust, and anger was picked up by other men, however, so most guys stayed clear of Jennifer. This avoidance only reinforced her belief that guys do not want to get close, especially to her. One of the results was that Jennifer became involved in a love relationship with a woman, which developed into a few sexual encounters. Now she was convinced that on top of everything else, she was homosexual. That's tough for a Christian!

We began to work together on Jennifer's prayer life. Instead of merely asking God to take away her sexual feelings toward women, I encouraged her to share her feelings with God. She began: "Lord, I feel so guilty about what I've done sexually with another woman. I know what I've done is against Your will and I'm scared to death that You will cut me off or punish me . . . that You already have . . . that You've given me up for no good." (She began to sob.)

I prayed silently that Jennifer would continue and express some of her anger as well. She went on: "Oh, Jesus, I'm so mad at my father . . . I could kill him! He has wrecked my mother's life. Sometimes I hate him! I know I shouldn't feel that way, but I do! But Mom made a choice too, Lord. She goaded him, threw away his liquor bottles, embarrassed him in front of friends. She figured she either had to do that or she never would stand up to him. I had to stand up to him too. I'm so mad I could scream." (Again Jennifer wept.)

At this point you may be asking, "Why all this catharsis?" Remember in chapter 1, where I discussed Dr. Larry Crabb's "layer theory"? On the outer two "layers" of a person's personality we find symptoms and emotions (feelings). We first need to deal with these two parts before moving in to a person's volitional self (behavior) and rational self (his thoughts). So I was helping Jennifer see that before she could get very far in her prayer life and in changing her thoughts, she needed to encounter God directly in conversational prayer. That is, she probably needed to tell God about her feelings.

Once Jennifer had expressed her rage, fear, and guilt, her personal self (thinking center) began to operate more clearly. She prayed: "And yet I know the past is over. Not all men are like my father was. All men are *not* alcoholics. Mom must have stayed with Dad for a reason. I know that I'm a big girl now and I no longer have to be at the mercy of others. The world *isn't* fair, but God, You are with me in the unfairness."

But, of course, her transition from fear, anger, and guilt wasn't that simple. Many times I encouraged Jennifer to pray out loud in my office, gently pushing her to express her feelings to the Lord. There was more anger, more tears, fear, and guilt. But each time this happened her emotions were more tempered. Jennifer's forgiving nature became more apparent. She was beginning to see life in a new perspective.

Listening to the Lord

A few years back I was jogging during the noon hour in order to blow off some of the pressure of hearing people's problems all day. As I often do while running or walking, I began to pray. Quite sometime ago I learned that, for me at least, conversational prayer is most helpful. While running that day it occurred to me that perhaps I was just having a one-way communication with God. What would happen, I thought, if I listened to what God had to say in return? God speaks to all of His children. Just as in human contacts, we often fail to hear Him because we don't listen.

Though some, like Paul in times past, and Michael Esser in modern times, hear Jesus' audible voice, to most of us He speaks through a still, small voice as he did to Elijah. All that is required of us is to listen. So I did. I prayed something like this: "Lord, I've given my life to You. And it is my commitment and desire for You to control my words, my thoughts, ideas, moods, impulses, desires, dreams, fantasies, and plans. Lord, I'm listening to You now. What do You want me to think about today. What do You want me to do?"

Then I waited. Some thoughts came to my mind: *You'll make it OK. Cheer up! Offer what you have to people. Be a servant. Also, take time to relax and enjoy. Outline times with your boys and Karen. Start doing special things for her. Let her know in different ways that you love her. Be thankful. I really helped you with your second client today. Did you know that? I'm proud of you. You're helping many people.*

Hang in, even when you get discouraged. My hand is on your shoulder.

I received some encouragement, some exhortation, and some ideas as to what my priorities should be for that week. I felt uplifted and rather surprised. *Maybe God has more to say,* I thought. Since that brisk fall day outdoors, I have "listened to the Lord" on a fairly regular basis. And many times He has put important thoughts in my mind. He has pushed Bible passages into awareness that were most helpful. He has exhorted me with, *When are you going to stop just thinking and start doing?* He has offered encouragement and support when I needed it.

Now of course I can't always be sure that all the thoughts I get when praying are from the Lord. But I certainly believe that there is a strong potential and probability that if I ask God to speak to me during prayer and that if I'm open to His leading, I greatly increase the probability that the thoughts which come to me *will* serve God's purposes.

Here's another version of the same theme. Choose a time at approximately the same hour every day, when you can be fairly certain of being undisturbed for 10 minutes. Sit down with pen and paper. Offer a simple prayer to the Lord, affirming that you have given your whole life to Him and that it is your desire for Him to control your thoughts, fantasies, and imagination. Tell Him you are listening and ask Him to speak to you. Then write down whatever comes to your mind. Be sure to write. This keeps your mind from wandering. It also gives you a record you can look back on. Many times this record will give you "counters," "alternative ways of thinking," biblical teaching, and practical ways of acting on your Christian beliefs.

On one occasion my spirits were really down. I went into a prayertime just expressing some of my anger, disappointment, and discouragement. Then I asked God to let me know what He was thinking by giving me some thoughts. Here's what I wrote: *You are OK. I love you. Jesus Christ is your Lord. He will love you until the end of time, no matter what.*

Be good to yourself. Relax and enjoy. Love yourself. I'm speaking to you. Where are you going? STOP! LOOK! LISTEN! Organize for action. Plan your life. Don't just let it go. Risk. If you're hurting, tell people. Don't be so apprehensive. Give yourself a break. You're sharp! People are interested in you. They love you. Reach out. Prepare. Listen to Me every day. I've got some real gems for you. Do your best. That's all you can do. I'll take care of the rest.

I'm not strong on mysticism, but I believe that God at that time gave me some thoughts which were most encouraging. Listen to these words!

I love you.

Jesus Christ is your Lord.

He will love you until the end of time, no matter what.

If you're hurting, tell people.

Do your best. That's all you can do. I'll take care of the rest.

Whenever I get discouraged, I go back to this list of uplifting thoughts. They come right out of my own prayer life. Who says Christianity is not practical?

Meditation and Imagery

Sometime ago, at a conference, the speaker asked us to meditate. Here's what he said: "First, I'd like you to close your eyes and relax for a few minutes. I'd like you to tune out all the different sounds, the smells, and the movement going on around you, and I'd like you to relax. Close your hands and make good tight fists—both hands. Tighten your fists and keep them there and hold the tension. Now, let go and totally relax. If you still feel tension, send a message to your hands to relax. We are just letting the tension go from our bodies—from our lives—we're just sitting still.

"Now I'd like you to use that wonderful gift that God has given all of us—your imagination—and I'd like you to imagine yourself walking along the beach, early in the morning. Notice the sun, which is just beginning to come up above the horizon. As you're walking, you notice it's nice and warm. It's light, but the beach is deserted. You're enjoying yourself because you're barefooted. You're walking in the damp sand and it feels very good. You're taking a walk and you're thoroughly enjoying it. A little way ahead, you see a man walking in your direction. You still feel most relaxed. This man is dressed casually. He's walking slowly and He's enjoying Himself a great deal. And, suddenly, somehow you know it's Jesus and you're getting really excited at the possibility of meeting Him and being with Him for a few moments.

"You continue walking. You're nearly to Him and He surprises you beyond words because He lifts His hand and He has a big smile on His face. His expression is vibrant and alive. He calls you by your first name, and He asks you how you are. He turns and walks with you in the same direction that you had been going. He pays close attention to what you say and shows He is interested in you. He stops you for a moment. He puts His arms around you and He tells you that He loves you. He tells you that His arms are always around you. He shares with you that He is fully aware of your life and that He is delighted in you as a person. He tells you that all of your big questions of life have been answered and that your challenge now is to experience the wholeness of life and to respond as joyfully and lovingly as you can to yourself, to your family, to your friends, and to God. You get the strong feeling that He thoroughly knows you, cares about you, and understands you—and you can hardly believe it.

"You continue walking and Jesus says that He has greatly enjoyed this time with you, but He has to go in the other direction. You wave good-bye and you tell Him the best you can how good this experience has been for you. As He leaves and you watch Him go, the whole experience begins to hit you. You were talking face to face with Jesus. And He shared with you how He loves you and cares for you—and you can hardly contain yourself.

"You're still walking on the beach but you're walking faster and you begin to run and you throw your arms in the air and you shout. You have never felt this much joy. You are *filled* with joy! Now, I would like for you to slowly open your eyes.

What did you experience?"

Yes, what did *you* experience? Peace? Freedom from your burdens? Safety? Security? That He loves you the way you are? Great warmth? Excitement?

One of the hindrances of some people's enjoyment of life is busyness and doing so much that they don't stop to relax and visualize the presence of Jesus Christ in their lives and taste the delights that He has for them.

Do you see Jesus walking through your life and being present with you both in hurting times and happy times? The Word of God tells us, "Jesus Christ is always the same, yesterday, today, and forever" (Heb. 13:8, PH).

And the Apostle Paul wrote: "No condemnation now hangs over the head of those who are 'in' Christ Jesus. For the new spiritual principle of life 'in' Christ Jesus lifts me out of the old vicious circle of sin and death" (Rom. 8:1-2, PH).

One way to experience Jesus is to see Him in your mind's eye as beside you, with His hand on your shoulder, or His arms wrapped around you, in all circumstances.

Recently a woman came to me who was troubled with many fears. She was constantly saying to herself, though somewhat subconsciously, *I'm not worth anything. People are constantly evaluating me, and my judgment is no good.* Again, we utilized countering strategies, and some visual imagery techniques such as VCI and SP/SR, mentioned in chapter 4. Then we went to prayer and to healing of memories through meditation and imagery.

Lucy recalled one incident in which she had asked to use the car in order to take a close friend out for a movie. Lucy was 17 at the time, had a driver's license, and had earned an "A" in Driver's Education. But her father said he did not trust Lucy's judgment with the car, and that he would take Lucy and her friend to the movie and pick them up afterward. This was one of "hundreds" of such incidents where Lucy's judgment had been questioned by her father.

We went to prayer. I asked the Lord to help Lucy feel the old feelings, experience the pain, and imagine clearly what was said, what she saw, felt, heard, and thought. I called on the Holy Spirit to help her re-experience this situation, not as a 30-year-old woman, but as a 17-year-old.

Then she began to express and describe to the Lord what she was re-experiencing. In her prayer, the anger came out. Her feelings of embarrassment and inadequacy were expressed, perhaps as she would have liked to have done when she was 17.

Then I introduced the person of Jesus into the scene. I prayed, "Lord, help Lucy to encounter You now in that scene. Help her to know Your presence there with her. Now, put Your hand on her shoulder and help her tell her Dad what she would have liked to have said at 17, but couldn't."

At that point Lucy stated, "Dad, I know you don't believe that I have good judgment, but Dad, I really do! Jesus thinks I have good judgment and I want you to know that because Jesus believes in me, I do too!"

Then I asked Lucy to face Jesus and tell Him that she forgives Dad. I asked her to envision a rope between her and her dad. The rope represents the assumption that Dad has the power to make her think, *Lucy, you have poor judgment.* Then I asked her to let Jesus walk between Lucy and Dad and cut the rope. Finally, I asked her to hear Jesus saying, "I am your new rope. I believe in you Lucy. You have fairly sound judgment. Your Dad didn't mean to say directly, 'You are not worthy.' He was being over protective. He was afraid. Can you see him as afraid, Lucy? I've forgiven him, Lucy, and I want you to forgive him too. And then grab onto your new rope!"

This process opened a door for Lucy. In her own imagination she experienced acceptance in light of some new thoughts, some new perspectives. Lucy grabbed tightly to this kind of prayer and during the next week she envisioned and prayed through several other similar experiences from her past. Each time she introduced the figure of Jesus and allowed Him to act in ways that fit His personality. She would see Him encouraging her to speak up, gently nudging her to believe in her judgment because He was behind her. At times Lucy would envision Jesus reminding her of a biblical truth, telling her that it was God's real truth.

Using Prayer and Meditation

How can you use the experiences described in this chapter? For one, try conversational prayer, as Jennifer did. Express your innermost feelings, cravings, desires, pain, joy, hope, anger, and sorrow directly to God. Do this as you would with a close friend. As you do I believe you will notice yourself putting situations more into perspective. The Lord will help you think more clearly as you express your emotions.

Secondly, utilize the methods I've described under the subhead, "Listening to the Lord." Try doing this daily, for at least two weeks, before possibly giving it up. Many people who do this report a much richer prayer life and a greater objectivity about life's problems.

Third, experience the beach scene with Jesus (page 49) for yourself. Make it as real as your imagination will allow. Encounter Him as you would a very close friend. Sense, at the same time, that He is God, the Messiah, the Lord of all! Then begin to pray through some of the painful episodes you've gone through in the past. Bring Jesus into the scene. Let Him minister to you in that encounter. Have Him put His hand in yours, or His arm around your shoulder. Tell Him what you would have liked to have told Him then, but couldn't—or didn't. Know that He has forgiven you and others in those situations. Realize that He wants you to forgive you, or your dad, or mother, sister, brother, friend, or in-law. Perceive a letting go of your burden from the past. Discern the Lord's truth for you in that situation and write it down. Refer to this truth often. Jesus is for real. Experience His healing!

6
Thinking Your Way Out of Depression

Depression is a pervasive problem in our country. One out of every eight persons can be expected to require treatment for depression in his lifetime. In milder form, practically everyone suffers from depression sooner or later. For example, you may stand so long in front of your closet trying to decide what to wear that you're ashamed. Or you may want to cry, but you can't. Or you may be overdrawn at the bank and can't help crying from the endless frustration of being short of money. Or you start waking up around 4:30 A.M. when it's still dark; that grainy dead-of-night dark. And you know you'll lie there, terrified and hopeless, while the dragon of depression whispers: "You blew it," or, "You should have known better," or, "What difference does it make?"

What Is Depression?
Perhaps the quickest way to understand what depression looks like is to describe its presence in another person. Several biblical people experienced depression firsthand. One of them was Moses. Several times while leading the Israelites in the wilderness, Moses became discouraged. His people were constantly complaining about how awful things were, and how they wished Moses had never led them out of Egypt.

54

Moses described his feelings of depression: Moses asked the Lord, "Why pick on me, to give me the burden of a people like this? Are they *my* children? Am I their father? Is that why You have given me the job of nursing them along like babies until we get to the land You promised their ancestors? Where am I supposed to get meat for all these people? For they weep to me saying, 'Give us meat!' I can't carry this nation by myself! The load is far too heavy! If You are going to treat me like this, please kill me right now; it will be a kindness! Let me out of this impossible situation!" (Num. 11:11-15, LB)

What was Moses experiencing? For one thing, he had lost hope. He felt he could not go on. He'd rather die than have to put forth any more effort. He was in despair.

Second, he had lost his perspective. He was not thinking clearly because he couldn't see the forest for the trees. He could not figure out any possible solutions.

Third, he had a strong desire to escape and withdraw from life. He cried, "Let me out of this impossible situation!"

Fourth, he was angry, both at God and at the Israelites. We can hear his anger in these statements: "Where am I supposed to get meat for all these people?" and "I can't carry this nation by myself!"

Fifth, he was feeling too dependent. He wanted someone else to come up with the answers. Most of Moses' complaints in this passage were in the form of questions that he put to God. He just didn't know how to go on with the everyday tasks of his life.

And, sixth, he was feeling inferior. This is seen in the last four sentences.

From the Prophet Elijah we can learn more about depression, its causes, and how it can be dealt with. You can read in detail about a depressed period in his life in 1 Kings 18 and 19. Let me highlight parts of it for you. Beginning in 1 Kings 18:41, we have the onset of events which probably contributed to Elijah's later despondency. First, he climbed up Mt. Carmel during mealtime. Then, he climbed back down the mountain and raced, on foot, for 20 miles, ahead of the king's chariots. Then Queen Jezebel threatened his life.

The result? Elijah was scared, physically exhausted, hungry, and probably worried a lot about the threat to his life. Soon he thought that everyone, including God, had deserted him. Then he did a peculiar thing. Instead of gathering friends around him, of which he had many, we are told that Elijah "went on alone into the wilderness, traveling all day [becoming still more exhausted], and sat down under a broom bush and prayed that he might die. 'I've had enough,' he told the Lord, 'Take away my life. I've got to die sometime, and it might as well be now.'"

Elijah had experienced several causes of depression: Insufficient rest, physical exhaustion, poor diet, isolation from friends, irrational negative thinking, self-pity. He had brought them on himself.

How did God deal with Elijah, in order to lift his depression? The Lord did not criticize Elijah for his depression. Too many times in Christian circles we do this. God certainly did not tell Elijah that being depressed was sinful. Instead, He sent an angel to minister to Elijah. The prophet slept and was given food. He was encouraged by God to talk about his depression. The prophet opened up, telling God about his concerns and worries.

Then God did a couple of things. First He reminded Elijah of his faulty thinking concerning the number of friends he had: "And incidentally, there are 7,000 men in Israel who have never bowed to Baal nor kissed him!" (19:18) God also urged Elijah to get into action (to counteract his apathy and despair). He was giving Elijah the realistic hope he could actually do something about his depression. And, with God's help, Elijah did.

Symptoms and Causes

Based on these two biblical accounts, about Moses and Elijah, we can identify several symptoms and causes of depression. Since the purpose of this book is not to diagnose, but instead to offer possible solutions, I will merely list symptoms and causes of depression and then move on to strategies.

What are a few symptoms that might signal you that you are depressed? If you answer, "Yes, much of the time" to most of the following statements you are probably depressed.

1. I feel downhearted and blue.
2. My life is not full.
3. I have trouble sleeping at night.
4. I do not enjoy the things I used to.
5. I have crying spells or feel like it.
6. Morning is when I feel the worst.
7. I feel that others would be better off if I were dead.
8. I eat much less than I used to.
9. I am losing weight.
10. I feel that I am useless and unneeded.
11. I find it difficult to make decisions.
12. I feel hopeless about the future.
13. My heart beats faster than usual.
14. I get tired fast, for no reason.
15. I find it difficult to do the things I used to.
16. I am restless and can't keep still.
17. I am more irritable than usual.
18. I no longer enjoy sex very much.
19. I have lost interest in other people.
20. I feel that I look worse than I used to.
21. I feel like a failure.
22. I feel very guilty.
23. I have thoughts of killing myself.

If you've answered over half of these in the affirmative, it is likely that you are experiencing some mood disturbance, some depression. If you answered yes to numbers 7 and 23, please see a trained professional counselor to evaluate your problems.

Or if you agree with all or almost all of these statements you may be moderately to severely depressed. Again, see a trusted and qualified counselor.

What about the causes of depression? There are many

potential causes. Here are a few:

1. Experiencing a loss through death, divorce, loss of a job, loss of a limb, etc.
2. Poor diet
3. Not enough sleep or rest
4. Anger that is repressed
5. Reactions to drugs
6. Physical causes, e.g., hypoglycemia (low blood sugar), infections of the brain or nervous system, general body infections, hepatitis, hormonal irregularities, either a hypo- or hyperthyroid condition. See a physician, especially if depression comes on suddenly for no apparent reason.
7. Physical exhaustion
8. Guilt
9. Faulty thought life

As we proceed further, it is important to remember that number 9, "Faulty thought life," is a principal cause for much depression today. In fact, it is on this cause that we will concentrate. However, the other eight causes are also important ones to consider, if you are feeling depression.

Use Your Counters

A negative thought life, as I've discussed in the first three chapters, can raise havoc with your spirits. A young man, Jim, came to me for help. He was in a blue funk. His wife was having an affair. Certainly, he had reason to feel bad! We talked about his pain, his rage, his guilt, his despair. There is no way such an episode can be lightly dismissed with a few prayers and a nice Scripture passage. First, Jim had to express his agony, his defeat.

Then I asked Jim to begin monitoring and writing down his automatic thoughts. His self-statements centered around three themes:

1. DEVALUATING SELF: *I'm no good. I cannot hold onto a woman. There must be something very wrong with me. I must be completely undesirable, worthless!*
2. DEVALUATING THE SITUATION: *It's all over for me. Life is a*

complete waste. Nothing is worth doing. Why should I even get out of bed in the morning?

3. DEVALUATING PROSPECTS FOR THE FUTURE: *I'll never make it! I'll never amount to anything! Life is hopeless! Nobody will ever love me!*

These three themes are commonplace for people who are depressed. Watch for them. In this case, Jim and I began to challenge his automatic thoughts with counters such as: *Who says I'm no good? Jesus died for me, so I must be worth something! Other women have found me attractive in the past. In fact, last week I was approached by a woman who didn't know I was married. Life is not all over, even though it feels like it. I love my work; I'm a talented musician. My children love me. I have many friends who care about me. How do I know that nobody will ever love me in the future? Or how do I know my wife will even continue her affair? She is seeing a Christian counselor about all this, so she must have some doubts. But even without her, God has a future for me, though I don't feel like it right now.*

Jim attacked his automatic thoughts, using the note card strategy mentioned in chapter 3. He also made his times of feeling depressed a signal for him to write down his automatic thoughts and develop at least three counters for each self-defeating statement.

Some other counters that are helpful for depression:

I'm catastrophizing again!

That thought only hurts me and makes me more depressed. What good is it?

Give yourself a break! I'd better check out the facts.

I assumed that she didn't like it, but it could be just as possible that she did like it.

My worth is totally based on God's declaration that I am OK. Who am I to argue with God?

This feels bad, no doubt. I don't like it! It isn't what I wanted and gives me no pleasure. But my entire worth does not depend on it.

Even if I do lose my wife it does not mean that the world

has nothing meaningful left in it.

It's OK not to be perfect.

Thinking constructively will be more productive.

I can try to solve this problem. I'm not eternally stuck with it.

If I want things to change I will have to act.

In his excellent book, *Feeling Good*, Dr. David Burns lists several "cognitive distortions" which can lead to depression:

1. ALL OR NOTHING THINKING. You see things in black and white categories. If your performance falls short of perfect, you see yourself as a *total* failure. For example, an excellent speaker who received 2 negative evaluations out of 100 people told me, "Now I'm a total failure. I'm going to quit public speaking."

2. OVERGENERALIZATION. You see a single negative event as a never-ending pattern of defeat. A mother overreacted to her son's misbehavior by yelling at him and calling him "Dummy!" From that sad experience she concluded, "I am a lousy parent. I always have been and always will be." As a matter of fact, when I pushed her to evaluate that statement, she couldn't remember when the last time was that she had called any of her children a bad name.

3. MENTAL FILTER. You pick out a single negative detail and dwell on it exclusively so that your vision of all reality becomes darkened, like a drop of ink that discolors an entire beaker of water. Carolyn, mother of a teenage son, had focused so heavily on one fire-setting episode that her son had been involved in two years ago, that she missed all of the redeeming features that the boy had. She labeled him as a "schizoid" and predicted that he would be a problem from that day on. But gradually she began to realize that Darren had only set that one fire, and had been basically responsible ever since.

4. DISQUALIFYING THE POSITIVE. You reject positive experiences by insisting that for some reason or other "they don't count." In this way, you can maintain a negative belief that is contradicted by your everyday experiences.

5. JUMPING TO CONCLUSIONS. You make a negative interpretation, even though there are no definite facts that convincingly support your conclusion. One example of this is "mind reading." You arbitrarily conclude that someone is reacting negatively to you, and you don't bother to check it out. Another example is "the fortune teller error" where you anticipate that things will turn out badly, and you feel and act as if this were already an established fact.

6. EMOTIONAL REASONING. You assume that your negative emotions necessarily reflect the way things really are: *I feel it; therefore it must be true.*

7. SHOULD STATEMENTS. These are the typical "rules" and "tapes" we try to live by, some of which are destructive:
All men are the same.
Women are fickle and overemotional.
Never get angry; it's a sin!

8. LABELING AND MISLABELING. This is an extreme form of overgeneralization. Instead of describing your error or someone else's, you attach a negative label:
I'm a loser.
*He's a no-good jerk.**

Thinking about your own depressed thoughts as possible "cognitive distortions" is a helpful way to begin challenging self-defeating statements. After you have written down some of your automatic thoughts, go through Dr. Burns' list and see if you can identify the kinds of "distortions" you are using to make yourself depressed.

The Use of Scripture
Here are several passages you may find meaningful and helpful when you are blue:

Philippians 4:6-9	Luke 4:18
Psalm 147:3	2 Corinthians 7:6
Psalm 42:11	Psalm 27

*David D. Burns, *Feeling Good.* New York: Signet Books, 1980.

Isaiah 41:10	Psalm 121
Psalm 43:5	Acts 27
Psalm 40:1-2	2 Corinthians 12:7-10

Waylon Ward has written a useful study guide to Psalm 121 that has helped many of my clients in their struggles with depression:

1. Read Psalm 121 over several times out loud, changing the pronouns to make it more personal. (Instead of *you* and *your*, substitute the first-person pronouns *my* and *me*.)

2. On 4" × 6" cards, write out Psalm 121. Use a bright-colored card or piece of paper that will stand out against most backgrounds. Write it on at least five different cards and post them in the places where you spend most of your time each day. As you see the cards at different times of the day, read the psalm again. The idea is for you to spend as much time as possible meditating on this psalm. This should become a daily practice and will focus your thoughts on God's care and protection.

3. If there is a time, situation, or place that seems to bring out your fears the most, work especially hard to focus your thoughts on Scripture at that time, or in that place. Many people find the time just before they go to sleep or when they first awaken each morning the most difficult of the day. Meditate on this psalm particularly at such times. Your bedside table should always have one of these cards on it.

4. Often when our minds are idle, our fears come rushing in. Try to meditate on this psalm when you find your mind free from other pressing details. Also, you might practice letting your fears remind you of this psalm. Memorize it. Any fearful thoughts you have can become springboards to meditation as you let the first fear or worry remind you of this comfort in God's Word.*

You can follow this same procedure with other Bible passages that are meaningful to you.

---

*Waylon Ward, *The Bible in Counseling*. Chicago: Moody Bible Institute, 1977.

Dick Dickinson of Inter-Community Counseling Center, Long Beach, California, has done a beautiful paraphrase of 1 Corinthians 13:4-8. I have found his statement to not only be of help with others, but I have found it personally helpful as well.

BECAUSE GOD LOVES ME
1 Corinthians 13:4-8

Because God loves me He is slow to lose patience with me.

Because God loves me, He takes the circumstances of my life and uses them in a constructive way for my growth.

Because God loves me, He does not treat me as an object to be possessed and manipulated.

Because God loves me, He has no need to impress me with how great and powerful He is because *He is God*, nor does He belittle me as His child in order to show me how important He is.

Because God loves me, He is for me. He wants to see me mature and develop in His love.

Because God loves me, He does not send down His wrath on every little mistake I make, of which there are many.

Because God loves me, He does not keep score of all my sins and then beat me over the head with them whenever He gets the chance.

Because God loves me, He is deeply grieved when I do not walk in the ways that please Him because He sees this as evidence that I don't trust Him and love Him as I should.

Because God loves me, He rejoices when I experience His power and strength and stand up under the pressures of life for His name's sake.

Because God loves me, He keeps on working patiently with me even when I feel like giving up and can't see why He doesn't give up on me too.

Because God loves me, He keeps on trusting me when at times I don't even trust myself.

Because God loves me, He never says there is no hope for me. Rather He patiently works with me, loves me, and disciplines me in such a way that it is hard for me to understand the depth of His concern for me.

Because God loves me, He never forsakes me, even though many of my friends might.

Because God loves me, He stands with me when I have reached the rock bottom of despair, when I see the real me and compare that with His righteousness, holiness, beauty, and love. It is at a moment like this that I can really believe that God loves me.

Yes, the greatest of all gifts is God's perfect love!

—Dick Dickinson

7

Stress and Anxious Thoughts

Jay's wife had just announced she was having an affair with a prominent professional in the community. She wanted to move out the following weekend and was not open to any convincing otherwise from Jay, their pastor, Christian friends, or her therapist. On top of that, Jay had just been chewed out by his boss that afternoon and had found 12 hits of "acid" in his teenage son's dresser drawer. Needless to say, when Jay called me he could have been pried off the ceiling with a spatula! His breathing was shallow. He was making little sense over the phone. On the one hand he wanted to run away to Acapulco and never return. On the other hand he pictured himself "going crazy" and wanting to be locked up in a mental health institute in the hope that he would suffer from eternal amnesia. He also had some thoughts of suicide, homicide, and you name it!

I listened to his panic and finally we moved toward talking about alternative actions he could take. Jay decided to confiscate the "acid" from his son. We role-played what he might say to his boss the next day. And, finally, he consented to make an appointment the following day to talk more about his marriage.

Stress is an everyday fact of life. You can't avoid it. Stress results from nearly every change that you must adjust to. And change is a fact of life in our times. While you usually think of stressful events as being negative, such as an injury, illness, or death of a loved one, a stress-producing situation may also be positive. For example, purchasing a new home or getting a promotion brings with it the stress of change of status and new responsibilities. A new addition to the family can put a strain on the family tie. Falling in love can be as stressful as falling out of love.

Stress

For years Jim drove himself to get ahead in his job as an advertising account executive. The pressures to compete for new accounts and to keep existing accounts were constant. Jim worked hard and long, partly because he had a mortgage and three children to put through college.

He was elated when he was made a vice-president of the firm. Then the pressures increased more and he worked even longer hours. His wife nagged him because she hardly ever saw him. He started drinking more and had periodic bouts of hypertension. Jim's doctor told him to slow down, but Jim said he couldn't. Then a year ago his wife died of cancer, and he couldn't cope with his job anymore. So, Jim was demoted. Six months later he was hospitalized because of a heart attack.

Stress. It has become as common as a cold and it is just as hard to avoid and more difficult to get rid of.

While some medical experts say that too much stress can make you ill, others go further and say it can kill you. It has been pinpointed by many as a contributing factor in hypertension, cancer, upset stomachs, insanity, nervous breakdowns, depression, headaches, colitis, allergies, skin disorders, heart disease, arthritis, rheumatism, and ulcers. The ill effect of stress is no respecter of age, socioeconomic status, or race. Everyone experiences stress daily, such as frustration in traffic, worrying over job pressures, or fear that a dinner party won't come off right.

Holmes-Rahe Stress Test*

One of the first steps in reducing stress is to become aware of the major sources of stress in your life. Though you are probably aware of the major ongoing environmental stresses in your life, you are likely to underestimate how many stressful changes occur every day to which you are forced to adjust. In order to become aware of the amount of stress you have had in the last year, please fill out and then score the following "Holmes-Rahe Stress Test." This was prepared by Thomas Holmes, M.D. at the University of Washington School of Medicine, Seattle, Washington.

HOLMES-RAHE STRESS TEST*
In the past 12 months, which of these have happened to you?

EVENT	VALUE	SCORE
Death of spouse	100	_____
Divorce	73	_____
Marital separation	65	_____
Jail term	63	_____
Death of close family member	63	_____
Personal injury or illness	53	_____
Marriage	50	_____
Fired from work	47	_____
Marital reconciliation	45	_____
Retirement	45	_____
Change in family member's health	44	_____
Pregnancy	40	_____
Sex difficulties	39	_____
Addition to family	39	_____
Business readjustment	39	_____
Change in financial status	38	_____
Death of a close friend	37	_____
Change in number of marital arguments	35	_____

*Thomas H. Holmes and Richard Rahe, "Stress Rating Scale," *Journal of Psychosomatic Research*, 1967, Vol. II, p. 216.

Mortgage or loan over $10,000	31	_____
Foreclosure of mortgage or loan	30	_____
Change in work responsibilities	29	_____
Son or daughter leaving home	29	_____
Trouble with in-laws	29	_____
Outstanding personal achievement	28	_____
Spouse begins or starts work	26	_____
Starting or finishing school	26	_____
Change in living conditions	25	_____
Revision of personal habits	24	_____
Trouble with boss	23	_____
Change in work hours, conditions	20	_____
Change in residence	20	_____
Change in schools	20	_____
Change in recreational habits	19	_____
Change in church activities	19	_____
Change in social activities	18	_____
Mortgage or loan under $10,000	18	_____
Change in sleeping habits	16	_____
Change in number of family gatherings	15	_____
Change in eating habits	15	_____
Vacation	13	_____
Christmas season	12	_____
Minor violation of the law	11	_____
TOTAL		_____

The more change points you have, the more likely you are to contract some sort of stress illness. Of those people with a score of over 300 for the past year, almost 80 percent get sick in the near future. With a score of 150 to 299, about 50 percent get sick in the near future. And, with a score of less than 150, only about 30 percent get sick in the near future. So the higher your score, the harder you will need to try to stay well.

Prevention
In order to make good use of this "stress test," follow these suggestions:

1. Become familiar with the life events and the amount of change they require.

2. Put the test where your family can see it easily.

3. Become aware when "life changes" occur and take note of them.

4. Allow yourself some time to express and experience some of the feelings and meaning of each life change as it occurs.

5. Think of alternative ways you can respond and adjust to each life change.

6. Think through any "life changes" that you plan to make before making them.

7. If possible, anticipate your life changes and plan for them well in advance.

8. Pace yourself. Try to control your number of life changes each year.

The Effects of Anxiety

Wayne Dyer, a well-known author and lecturer, has stated: You could take the 10 best worriers in the entire world. Put them in the same room for the rest of their lives and allow them to worry and worry only. And you know what would happen? Absolutely nothing!

God's Word has some things to say about the effects of worry and anxiety: "I heard, and my [whole inner self] trembled, my lips quivered at the sound. Rottenness enters into my bones and under me—down to my feet—I tremble (Hab. 3:16, AMP).

The proverbist wrote, "Anxiety in a man's heart weighs it down" (Prov. 12:25, AMP). This certainly describes the feelings that anxious individuals relate to me in my counseling office. They actually feel as if there is a heaviness pushing down on their bodies. They feel helpless and overwhelmed.

There are physiological effects as well. Anxiety causes people to experience headaches, backaches, increased perspiration, weakness and fatigue, shortness of breath, constriction in the chest, indigestion, butterflies in the stomach, diarrhea, "pounding heart," menstrual irregularity, insomnia, and muscular tension.

When we are anxious, our attention is impaired and our mental activities are interfered with. We have poor concentration and judgment. There is a good deal of interference with the efficiency and effectiveness of our mental functioning, especially as tasks become more complex. So our important problem-solving skills are reduced to a minimum when we are highly anxious.

An old Moorish proverb states, "He who is afraid of a thing gives it power over him." Worry and fear can become self-fulfilling prophecies. Job said, "For what I fear comes upon me, and what I dread befalls me" (Job 3:25). Statistics show that if you are the type of person who worries about having accidents, you are a more likely candidate for such a mishap.

One speechmaker asks, "What if I forget what my notes mean? What if they ask a question I can't answer? What if they start complaining about my speech? What if some of them fall asleep?"

Another person says, "I'm nervous about this speech, but that's normal. I've yet to meet someone who says that he does not get anxious about giving a talk. I'm well prepared. I'll just take my time, tell them what I know, and go from there."

Which one do you suppose is the more successful public speaker?

Small Beginnings in Overcoming Anxiety
Earl Nightingale, a business consultant, says that 40 percent of our worries are about things that never happen. Another 30 percent concern things that are in the past, which can't be changed by worry. Still another 12 percent are needless worries about our health. And 10 percent of our worries Nightingale designates as "petty, miscellaneous worries" not worth worrying about. That leaves a total of 8 percent for real legitimate concerns! So let's look at some ways to deal with the 92 percent of our illegitimate worries and anxieties.

Suzie had always experienced fear when she was around

groups of people. Ever since her junior high days Suzie believed she had too little going for her. At that time she was skinny, sported a set of braces, wore thick glasses, and never dared speak in class, or to any boys. Furthermore, Suzie's parents had strongly discouraged her from doing any dating until she was 18. A few times she attempted to offer some ideas in class, but her voice was so quiet and shaky that her peers giggled and the teacher merely passed over her after Suzie's third attempt to speak up.

All through high school Suzie avoided social gatherings, developed "stomach aches" in order to miss discussion-oriented classes, and stayed home weekends to do homework or watch television.

Later, somehow, she met and married Peter. Then Suzie was forced to attend parties and dinners for his company and their church. Yet she was still terrified. If you could have heard some of her automatic thoughts they would have gone something like this: *No one likes me. They think I have nothing to offer. And it's true. I don't have anything to offer. I don't meet other people's expectations of me. That's awful! I'll probably say something dumb or stupid. People know that I'm stupid! I'm sure I don't look as good as others either. I never could! Nobody will ever like me. I'll just mess up Peter's business contacts. I don't deserve him.*

In effect Suzie was saying, *What other people think of me is of such crucial importance that I must anticipate being rejected in advance of all my actions. I must do everything I can to prevent others from thinking badly of me. If they think badly of me, it's all over. That would be awful.*

By *it's all over* Suzie meant, *There's nothing left in life for me.* The truth is that if we believed *there's nothing left in life* every time someone thought badly of us, life would soon be a big nothing for all of us.

Here are some words of truth which Suzie learned and used to argue against her self-defeating thoughts:

"This is the reason why we never collapse. The outward man does indeed suffer wear and tear, but every day the inward man receives fresh strength" (2 Cor. 4:16, PH).

"Behold, I give unto you power to tread on serpents and scorpions, and over all the power of the enemy; and nothing shall by any means hurt you" (Luke 10:19, KJV).

"Greater is He that is in you than he that is in the world" (1 John 4:4 KJV).

"They that wait upon the Lord shall renew their strength; they shall mount up with wings as eagles; they shall run, and not be weary; and they shall walk, and not faint" (Isa. 40:31, KJV).

"For God has not given us [me] a spirit of timidity, but of *power* and *love* and *discipline*" (2 Tim. 1:7).

"If God is for us, who is against us?" (Rom. 8:31)

It took Suzie days and weeks of memorization and repetition of these verses, plus meditating and acting on them, before she began to "mount up with wings like eagles."

Using Scripture

Suzie had learned to utilize God and His Word in helping herself overcome her intense fear and anxiety. She used the simple note card technique described in earlier chapters. On one side of a 3" × 5" note card she wrote the words STOP, GO AWAY, QUIT BUGGING ME! On the other side of the card she wrote out a Bible passage or two. She kept five or six cards with her at all times. Whenever she began to worry, Suzie would pull out a card or two, or all six. She read the word STOP, which meant "Stop thinking this way!" She said it aggressively. If alone, Suzie would say, "Quit bugging me!" out loud. If she were with people Suzie would scream internally, *Go away, dumb thoughts!* Then she would turn her cards over and read those beautiful verses. She relished each word as she read it. Suzie allowed the truth of those words to really sink in. She was punishing or breaking the chain of worry by giving herself the cue to STOP. Then she replaced her anxiety and irrational thoughts with some alternative thinking from the Lord.

Here are some passages that you can use with the same

note card technique. Remember, only use a passage that speaks directly to you. Use a translation of the Bible that you can really relate to. (For some passages I've made suggestions as to which translation or paraphrase might be most meaningful.)

1 Peter 5:7 (NASB)	Isaiah 26:3 (LB)
Psalm 37:1, 3-5, 7 (AMP)	Matthew 6:34 (LB)
Proverbs 15:15 (AMP)	Psalm 121
Psalm 34 (LB)	Psalm 4:8
Isaiah 41:10 (NASB)	Psalm 23
Isaiah 43:2-3 (NASB)	Philippians 4:4-9
Romans 5:1 (LB)	Isaiah 43:1 (NASB)
John 16:33 (LB)	

Prayer

In a book titled *The Edge of Adventure*, I came across what has been for me a godsend in my own prayer life. The authors outline "Seven minutes of time with God." In the first 30 seconds you just try to relax. Take a deep breath and realize that God, who loves you deeply, is there with you. Ask Him to calm your heart and make you receptive to His will. During the next 4 minutes, you read in the Gospel of John, not for factual information, but with two questions in mind:

1. What kind of personality does God, the One to whom I have given my life, have?

2. Is there anything here that speaks to me for today, now? During the last 2½ minutes of prayer the authors suggest the following order:

1. ADORATION. Just tell Christ that you love Him, in your own words. "I love You, Christ, I want to respond to You with my whole life." A line from a psalm may be another way to do this. Any expression of praise that comes from the depths of your soul often helps.

2. CONFESSION. What I do here is to lay out to God specific things that I am genuinely sorry for. I am most specific about what I'm asking forgiveness for.

3. THANKSGIVING. Again, I'm specific. This can be a beautiful time of searching for and discovering many of the blessings in my own life.

4. SUPPLICATION. First, I pray for others and their needs. And when I get to my own needs I have often prayed, "And as for me, Lord, Thy will be done." This simple statement, along with the "adoration" part of my prayertime, has helped me let go of my own anxieties and fears.*

I have often had my prayertime while I am beginning my day, while jogging and exercising. That puts some energy into it! Besides, it's also a way to make jogging more interesting.

Counters

If you have difficulty finding good counters for your anxiety-producing thoughts, here are some that have been helpful for others:

This thought only hurts me by making me panic.

All this excessive worry changes nothing!

This thought is pointless!

Nobody's perfect!

Cool it!

What am I doing to myself?

Everybody makes mistakes!

I can only do so much!

Tomorrow is another day.

I've done all I can.

Let go. Let God handle the rest.

Now wait a minute. Before I get carried away I need to think this through.

I'm in charge of my own head. I'll decide whether I'll panic or not.

"Do not fear, for I am with you; do not anxiously look about you, for I am your God. I will strengthen you, surely I

---

*Adapted from *The Edge of Adventure: Response Manual,* Keith Miller and Bruce Larson. Waco, Texas: Creative Resources, 1974, p. 78.

will help you. Surely I will uphold you with My righteous right hand!" (Isa. 41:10)

"I have called you by name; you are Mine! When you pass through the waters, I will be with you; and through the rivers, they will not overflow you. When you walk through the fire, you will not be scorched, nor will the flame burn you. For I am the Lord your God" (Isa. 43:1-3).

What metaphors Isaiah uses! God says, "I will be with you . . . through the rivers." In the summer I do a lot of stream fishing for trout in the Colorado Rockies. I know how the force of a deep cold current can knock over a large man in an instant, filling his waders and rendering him helpless in the waters of the river. God is saying, in effect, "When your waders are filled to your hips with water and the currents of life are dragging you down and under, you will *not* be overwhelmed, if you grab My victorious right hand." And I'm certain that the God who created the vast powers of solar and interplanetary forces has a rather powerful right hand!

8
Guilt: Destructive and Not So Destructive

Bob had many skills. He was asked by his pastor to serve as an elder on the church board. He was already helping out by volunteering to sit on the finance committee of their branch mission church. But he sensed that he dare not say no to being on the board. What would others say if he refused? He just didn't feel he had the option to turn his pastor down. After all, he had confessed his beliefs to be real. He was a Christian! But Bob was already serving on several other committees. He wanted more time for his family, but could he turn down being an elder in his church?

Over the next few years Bob was absent from his family on Sunday nights. There were emergency meetings on Saturdays, Sunday afternoons, Monday nights. His wife, Christine, began to complain. His son, Kirk, began to act up. At a school conference the counselor had asked Bob if he could spend more time with Kirk. Good idea! But when? Bob's schedule was so jam-packed that the only way they could meet would be for Kirk to make an appointment with him! Bob began to feel resentment and anger toward his church. He viewed his involvement there with disgust and bitterness. Not only was he ineffective at home, but his contribution to the church board became marginal at best.

Guilt struck again!

Recognizing Guilt

If you feel sad, depressed, downcast, unhappy, self-blaming, or self-condemning, it is possible that real guilt lurks underneath your surface. A new Christian came to see me recently. He had been involved in a sexual affair with a Christian woman who had decided that God would overlook their sin. One of the biggest causes of this man's depression was his guilt over this sexual entanglement. He was also consumed with guilt because he had divorced his wife a year ago.

If there are "hidden subjects" that you would not want anyone to know and have never told anyone, guilt may be weighing you down. Some time ago a middle-aged woman came to me for counseling. She was depressed and anxious. For eight years she had been sitting on overwhelming guilt feelings concerning two abortions she had had. She was so ashamed of what she had done that it took six counseling sessions before she would tell me about the abortions. With that confession came floods of tears. She had never told anyone before. And because she had kept her feelings private, Connie worked on herself daily. She told herself, *I am just plain evil. I'm no good. God would never want me! Having two abortions is the worst thing any human can do! It just proves how stupid I am. No one would want me around if they knew.* So Connie stayed away from people. She stayed away from God too. For eight years she holed herself up in her apartment and would not allow anyone to become emotionally close to her.

Another possible clue that guilt may be a problem with you is your attitude toward others who sin. If you find yourself condemning others for wrongdoing, take heed. It is highly likely that you come down pretty hard on yourself as well. An attractive young lady presented her problem as depression. I began to see that perfectionism and its accompanying guilt was highly instrumental in creating her depression. Any time others did not live up to Peggy's expectations, she would secretly denounce them. And whenever Peggy did not meet her own standards she would denounce herself.

Unrealistic generosity may be another sign of guilt. I have a friend who is constantly offering his services for this and that. I've come to know that half of the services he offers he could never follow through on, and he doesn't. Interestingly a month ago he confessed to me that his life was stained with immoral acts and he was trying desperately to make up for them by being helpful to others.

According to David Burns, guilt is the emotion you will experience when you have the following thoughts:

1. I have done something I shouldn't have (or I have failed to do something that I should have) and my actions fall short of my moral standards and violate my concept of fairness.

2. This "bad behavior" shows that I am a bad person (or that I have an evil streak, or a tainted character, or a rotten core, etc.).*

Remorse Vs. Guilt

It's the concept of the badness of self that is central to guilt. Remorse is different from guilt in that remorse is aimed at a change in behavior. Guilt is aimed at the self. The difference between remorse and guilt is illustrated in the Parable of the Prodigal Son. Seeing that his rebellion had not helped himself or anyone else, the prodigal son changed his behavior and returned home to his father and upright living. He was remorseful. According to this definition of guilt, if the prodigal son had merely labeled himself as "bad" and "hopeless" he might have acted quite differently. He might well have figured that he was completely unworthy to return home. He might have remained stuck in his immoral behavior, thinking such thoughts as:

I am worthless. Others look down on me. I should be severely punished for my wrongdoing. No one would forgive me. No one should forgive me. I deserve to live forever with the hogs and the filth I'm in.

The woman who had had two abortions had made the

---

*David Burns, *Feeling Good*. New York: Signet, 1980, p. 178.

decision that she deserved everlasting punishment. Judas decided the same thing after he betrayed Jesus. Countless others who have groveled in self-pity became alcoholics, or fell into the grips of depression, or committed suicide. Basically they have all decided, "I deserve to live forever with the hogs and the filth I'm in."

You see, for a member of God's family it's not so bad to admit, "I blew it! I fell short. I need to ask for forgiveness. I need to say I'm sorry, both to that other person and to God."

But to grovel in self-blame and call yourself a "worm" is not necessary or desirable. This is illustrated so well by Jesus' attitude toward a woman taken in adultery (John 8). Jesus did *not* say to this woman, "I want you to go home and think about what a horrible person you are." He did not suggest that she be stoned or condemned. He did not tell her she was a "worm" or a "slut" or a "whore." He turned to her and said, "Go, and sin no more." He was telling her to suffer from remorse, not guilt. He was saying, "Learn from your misdeed; change your direction; do something more constructive next time."

Not once does the Bible encourage believers in Jesus Christ to accept psychological guilt. Not once are Christians commanded to have a fear of punishment, a sense of worthlessness, or a feeling of rejection. In fact, of the three New Testament Greek words translated "guilt" in English (*enochos, hupodikos,* and *opheilo*), not one refers to a *feeling* of guilt. Instead, they mean "to owe or be indebted to," "to be liable to judgment," and "to be guilty of an offense."

We need to realize that if we are trusting in Christ, God will not punish us for our confessed sins. He punished Christ in our place. But God does *correct* or *discipline* us. This is entirely different. Punishment is a payment for misdeeds, and Christ made that payment nearly 2,000 years ago. Now God only corrects us as a loving Father. God instructs us to change our behavior. He may do this through feedback from a friend or in the form of a convicting sermon. Or perhaps He speaks to us while we're reading Scripture, or during our prayertime. Yet His purpose is not to punish us or put us down. His purpose is to correct us.

Bruce Narramore and Bill Counts suggest that God *disciplines* Christians, but may choose to *punish* a non-Christian to make him aware of his need for God.* A comparison of the following biblical passages illustrates the great difference between God's punishment and His discipline.

TO THE CHRISTIAN (DISCIPLINE): "My son, do not despise the Lord's discipline and do not resent His rebuke, because the Lord disciplines those He loves, as a father the son he delights in" (Prov. 3:11-12, NIV).

TO THE NON-CHRISTIAN (PUNISHMENT): "Behold, the Day of the Lord is coming, cruel, with fury and burning anger, to make the land a desolation; and He will exterminate its sinners from it. . . . Thus I will punish the world for its evil, and the wicked for their iniquity; I will also put an end to the arrogance of the proud, and abase the haughtiness of the ruthless" (Isa. 13:9, 11).

TO THE CHRISTIAN (DISCIPLINE): "All those whom I love I correct and discipline. Therefore, shake off your complacency and repent" (Rev. 3:19, PH). Incidentally, to *repent* in the New Testament always involves a change for the better. *Metanoia*, the Greek noun for repentance, refers to a change of mind involving both a turning from sin and a turning to God. The following chart summarizes what I've been saying.**

	PUNISHMENT	DISCIPLINE
Purpose	To inflict penalty for an offense, to pay back for wrongs	To correct and promote positive growth
Focus	Past misdeeds	Future correct deeds

---

*Bruce Narramore and Bill Counts. *Freedom from Guilt*. Vision House: Santa Ana, Calif., 1974.
**Narramore and Counts, *Freedom From Guilt*, p. 72.

Attitude	Righteous anger	Love
Resulting emotion in the punished or disciplined person	Fear, guilt, and hostility	Security

As you can see, discipline's purpose is to correct and promote positive growth. It is future-oriented and is based on love and security. Punishment, on the other hand, is based on fear and guilt, and its purpose is to pay back for wrongs. When we mess up and begin to clobber ourselves, aren't we treating ourselves in the way that God sometimes deals with non-Christians? Aren't we really internally saying things such as the following?

I'm bad, and I'll have to pay for that by getting some kind of punishment.

I am a raunchy person, a complete failure.

I don't deserve anything!

God can't love me anymore. I'm stained, wicked.

I'm of no worth to God or anyone.

What will everyone think of me?

If others found out what I did, they would all look down on me.

It's my fault that she is upset. I should never have criticized her.

A 10-year-old-girl, Susan, was to give a recital on her violin in two days. While practicing she left the instrument on a chair in the living room for a moment, while she hurried to the kitchen for a drink of water. In the meantime Susan's mother walked into the living room and without looking did you know what. Crunch! She sat right on Susan's violin. Screaming, yelling, blaming, self-blaming, and self-pitying statements flowed from Mom's mouth for about 10 minutes. Finally, when Mom ran out of words, Susan said, "Mom, I'm really sorry about what happened, but calling yourself and me names isn't going to help much. Right now we need to think about two things. One, how can we make sure this never happens again? Two, how can I find another violin for the recital on Saturday?"

Susan actually gave two beautiful counters for paralyzing one's guilt-laden thoughts:

1. *What can I do to prevent this from happening again (if the act was bad)?*

2. *What can I do that will help?*

Notice that neither of these two questions can be answered by blaming yourself or others. Nor can either question be answered with an expression of self-pity or putting yourself down.

Dealing with Guilt

One strategy for dealing with guilt relates back to "putting your thoughts on trial." Remember? We discussed this in chapter 3, "Countering: Arguing with Yourself." Let's say that you have just said something to a friend and she suddenly becomes very quiet and then changes the subject. Later you learn through the grapevine that what you said embarrassed and hurt your friend. You had no intention of hurting her, but it happened. We'll call this Situation A. Some of your B Statements or automatic thoughts could go like this:

I really hurt my friendship with Mary. What an idiot I am—always saying the wrong thing! I deserve her anger. I wouldn't blame her if she never spoke to me again!

One way to facilitate the process of "putting a thought on trial" is to state it in this form:

I should feel (the emotion) because (the situation). For example, *I should feel inferior because* I did not make the team.

Returning to the B Statements for hurting a friend, how might we restate these in the form, *I should feel (the emotion) because (the situation)?* How about this?

I should feel rotten because I accidentally hurt my friend's feelings.

Now, let's define what we mean by "rotten."

Rotten = worthless, no good.

Now, let's put the thought on trial. The thought is: *I should feel* "worthless and no good" *because* I accidentally hurt my friend's feelings. Remember the five methods for proving or disproving an automatic thought? They are:

1. Use your senses.
2. Ask an authority.
3. Find out what most people think.
4. Use your own reasoning and logic.
5. Use your own experience.

Let's use number 3, "Find out what most people think." What would most people think of the statement, *I should feel worthless and no good because I accidentally hurt my friend's feelings?*

My guess is that most people would say, "That's ridiculous!" Or, "You're being much, much too hard on yourself!" Or, "You're expecting absolute perfection of yourself!"

Refer to your cognitive distortions list. In chapter 6 we said that our depressed thoughts may be "cognitive distortions." Remember? Several of these "distortions" readily lend themselves to guilt. For example, "jumping to conclusions" is common. It is the assumption that you have done something terribly wrong when perhaps you really haven't.

Recently I became angry with my nine-year-old son, Cory, for something he had done. I read him the riot act. Then guilt set in. I jumped to the conclusion that what I did must have been terribly wrong because Cory seemed crushed. Later I checked out with my wife Karen, how she saw what I had done and said. She supported me, stating that she would have reacted in the same way. I also shared this episode with a friend at a breakfast meeting the next day, and he too supported my reaction toward Cory. Perhaps it was OK for Cory to hear how angry I was about what he had done. I didn't need to carry the burden of guilt.

I'm not saying here that people never behave badly. Certainly we do! Saying that we always do what's right is just as unrealistic as "jumping to conclusions." The point is we sometimes need to check out our reactions with others, using our own experience and logic, and also refer to authorities and Scripture.

Another common guilt-provoking distortion is "labeling." Instead of describing your error or someone else's, you attach a negative label:

I'm a loser.

He's a no-good jerk!

"Should statements" are another common pathway toward guilt. Some examples are:

I should never get angry; it's a sin.

I shouldn't have these sexual feelings; I'm dirty.

I should feel guilty because I said no to a request from a friend.

I should be happy at all times.

I should feel guilty because I asked for a favor.

Many of our "shoulds" come from what parents and others in authority have told us. Again, not all "shoulds" are self-defeating or nonsense. For example, "Thou shalt not steal" is a reasonable "should." It is designed to help, not hurt. And it's biblical.

But if your guilt and "should" statements are not helping you live more biblically, then what's the point? Remember, remorse is sorrow over a misdeed and leads to correction of the misdeed. But long-lasting and self-abusive guilt is simply not constructive.

Write down the advantages and disadvantages of believing the "shoulds." Let's say that you are telling yourself that you should be able to make your spouse happy all the time. What are the advantages and disadvantages of having that rule for yourself?

ADVANTAGES	DISADVANTAGES
1. I'll work hard to be a good husband (or wife).	1. I could become resentful, especially if my wife (husband) does not give as much in return.

2. I'll be continually giving to my mate.

2. My wife (husband) is depressed a lot. Her (his) unhappiness often has little to do with me, so no matter what I do, I sometimes fail to make her (him) happy.

3. My partner could act unhappy to get what he (she) wants. This would be manipulating me through my guilt.

Who says I should? Another "should" removal technique involves asking yourself the question, *Who says I should? Where is it written that I should?* Perhaps you have decided that being angry is a sin, and that you should feel guilty if you feel angry toward someone. In trying to answer the question, *Where is it written that I should feel guilty for being angry?* you search the Scriptures. You discover that Jesus was angry with the Pharisees on several occasions. You read about His irritation with His disciples when they fell asleep on Him at Gethsemane. You see how He seemed to lose His temper completely when He drove the money-changers out of the temple with a whip. You read the Psalms and hear David expressing anger directly toward God. You observe Moses even got angry with God, and so did Job. What does all this evidence suggest about our initial premise, *I should feel guilty because I sometimes get angry?*

Use your counters. Here are some counters for arguing against guilt-inducing automatic thoughts.

Who says I'm worthless

I can make a mistake but I'm not a mistake.

God wants me to experience remorse and repentance, but not long-lasting guilt.

What can I do better next time? That's the question.

How is this thought helping me change my behavior?

Who says I deserve to suffer?

Other people won't love and respect me more because I'm feeling guilty and putting myself down.

This thought simply does not fit reality.

It would be nice if *I could make my wife happy now because she seems upset. I can ask what she's upset about and see if I can help in some way.*

Why should I?

I'm not responsible for other people's feelings.

I can't make others feel the way they do.

What about real sin that I've committed? As Christians we have a resource to draw on to combat our guilt that a non-Christian does not have. We have the person of Jesus Christ. If we have real guilt, something to express realistic sorrow over, we can get rid of it by confessing it to our Lord. In Psalm 51 we see the dramatic feelings of guilt David experienced at one time. The Prophet Nathan had just informed David of God's judgment on him. David had committed adultery with Bathsheba. If that wasn't enough David also had Uriah, her husband, murdered so that He could marry Bathsheba. Here are some of David's feelings: "O loving and kind God, have mercy. Have pity upon me and take away the awful stain of my transgressions. Oh, wash me, cleanse me from this guilt. Let me be pure again. For I admit my shameful deed—it haunts me day and night!" (Ps. 51:1-3, LB)

David was down! He was consumed with guilt. And his guilt was real. He had done some pretty bad stuff. But in this psalm, he worked out his guilt by expressing his broken spirit, remorse, and penitence to God. Here is a model of what we should do with our guilt. We should confess it to our Lord, with broken and contrite hearts. If we do, He *will* forgive us!

If you are feeling an overwhelming sense of guilt, please share it with someone you can trust. Here are three steps you can take:

1. Express the depths of your remorse to God in prayer. Perhaps you may want to use the "beach scene," described in chapter 5, to help make this confession seem more real to you.

2. Go to a pastor or Christian counselor who believes in the value of confession and will hold your expressed guilt in confidence. Again pour out your feelings of guilt. Have the helping person pray with you concerning your misdeeds. Allow your feelings to pour out. They're real. They're OK. God accepts your feelings. The importance of accepting God's forgiveness cannot be overemphasized, nor can the genuine expression of your pain.

3. After you have confessed, take a step of faith and thank Christ Jesus for His forgiveness. Take a deep breath of air and let it out. As you release that breath of air, also let go of your guilt. If you have any recurrence of these guilt feelings, simply say silently, "Thank You, Jesus, for You have forgiven me." Then go on about whatever you are doing. Use this phrase as a counter to any nagging irrational doubts that God has forgiven you. In God's Word we have many assurances that we are forgiven our shortcomings. Jesus said, "Your sins are forgiven" (Luke 5:20). David wrote that "the Lord does not count against" His blessed ones their sin (Ps. 32:2, NIV). The Apostle Paul wrote, "While we were still sinners Christ died for us" (Rom. 5:8, NIV). Other passages which you may find helpful:

Romans 8:1
1 Corinthians 6:9-11
Ephesians 1:4
Colossians 1:14
Colossians 1:22
1 Peter 1:3
2 John 2:12

Waylon Ward has given us a helpful exercise in experiencing God's forgiveness. Use it. It's one of the most helpful assignments I've ever given to anyone who is consumed with guilt. It beautifully counters unproductive guilt.

Each passage should be read from at least two versions. Recommended Bibles include *New International Version, The Living Bible, Amplified Bible, and New American Standard Bible.*

1. Read 1 John 1:9. The word *confess* means to agree with God concerning your sin. It simply means acknowledge that you have sinned and that Jesus died for that sin too. What sin or sins do you acknowledge to God right now?

_____

_____

_____

2. What does 1 John 1:9 say God will do about your sins?

_____

_____

3. How much unrighteousness will God cleanse you from?

_____

4. Did you confess your sins?_____ Did God forgive

   you? _____ Are you now cleansed from all your

   unrighteousness?_____

5. Write out a brief prayer, thanking God for forgiving your

   sin and also for cleansing you._____

_____

_____

_____

6. Why can God forgive you and cleanse you of your sin?

(1 Peter 1:18-19; 2:24) _____

_____

_____

7. What is needed for forgiveness? (Heb. 9:22)_____

_____

8. For whose sins did Jesus die? (1 John 2:2)_____

9. What does God say He will do after you confess your sins?

   (Heb. 10:17-18)_____

_____

10. How far away have your sins been removed? (Ps. 103:12)

_____

11. How pure and clean does the Lord make you? (Isa. 1:18)

_____

12. How has God dealt with your sins? (Isa. 53:5-6)_____

_____

13. Read 1 Corinthians 6:9-10. Do any of the words listed

    there refer to you? _____ Which ones?_____

_____

These verses say that God has done three things for you.

What are these three things:

(a) _____

(b) _____

(c) _____

14. Read 2 Corinthians 5:21. Who took your sins?_____

    Whose righteousness did you receive?_____

15. How does God feel about you? (Zeph. 3:17)_____

    _____

    Read also Ephesians 1:11, 18 (in *The Living Bible,* if
    possible) and describe God's attitude toward you.

    _____

    _____

16. Read James 5:16. Why should we confess our sins to one

    another?_____

    _____

    Does this mean that you tell everybody about your sins?

    _____

    It means that you confess your sin to a righteous person
    who can and will pray for you, someone you really trust.
    Whom do you trust enough to confess your sins to?

    _____

    _____

Why do you go to that person? _____

_____

17. Read 1 John 1:7. What happens when you turn on a light

    in a dark room? _____
    Satan loves to keep things hidden because he can use them
    against you, but when you confess to a Christian friend you
    really trust it brings those hidden sins into the light of
    God's healing love. Satan hates that light.

9
Speaking the Truth in Love

Do you feel that people don't understand what you need or want from them? Do you find yourself avoiding disagreements at all costs? Are most of your days filled with disappointments, criticisms, and failures? When someone gives you a compliment, do you deny it? Would you like to make friends, but find it difficult to take the first step in doing so? Is it hard for you to say no to a request when you'd really rather not do what is asked? Do you find it difficult to talk about yourself in a positive way?

If you found yourself nodding your head vertically to some or most of these questions, this chapter is important for you.

Aggressive, Assertive, Passive
There are three general types of human behavior: aggressive behavior, assertive behavior, and passive behavior. If you answered yes to some or most of the above questions, you were expressing either an aggressive or passive manner of behavior.

Aggressive Behavior
What do I mean by aggressive? Let's say that you want a member of your family to clean the garage and you say, "I

suppose it would be too much to ask of your excellence to even put a finger on the broom and push it around the garage." That's an example of aggressive behavior. In making a request in this manner, you would be stepping on the other person's toes, ignoring his dignity, and failing to take his feelings into consideration. This way of communicating would also successfully alienate the other person. Instead of using his hands to push the broom around, he would probably like to place them tightly around your neck and squeeze!

All too often we fail to recognize that put-downs, name-calling, sarcasm, and coercion are only successful in alienating us from others. Part of the problem is that we recognize this fact only after the damage has been done and we've already blasted away. Scripture speaks of the power of our words: "But no one can tame the tongue; it is a restless evil and full of deadly poison. With it we bless our Lord and Father; and with it we curse men, who have been made in the likeness of God: From the same mouth come both blessing and cursing. My brethren, these things ought not to be this way" (James 3:8-10). "Death and life are in the power of the tongue" (Prov. 18:21). "How long will you torment me, and crush me with words?" (Job 19:2)

Adding to the dilemma is the fact that aggressive behavior is often rewarded. For example, the boss who screams at her secretary, "You'd better get this letter out today or else!" will probably see the finished letter on her desk, ready for signing within seconds. Thus, the secretary's quick response rewards the boss for stomping all over her secretary.

Or consider the father who constantly forces his children to do whatever he wants them to do, seldom taking their feelings or opinions into account. He will probably be rewarded initially for his aggressive, noncaring actions by his children's fearful compliance. But watch out later, when his children become older and he is no longer able to physically restrain them. Then they will rebel, either openly or quietly and surreptitiously.

Paul wrote to Christian parents at Ephesus: "Don't keep on

scolding and nagging your children, making them angry and resentful. Rather, bring them up with the loving discipline the Lord Himself approves, with suggestions and godly advice" (Eph. 6:4, LB).

We know for certain, from psychological research and from every indication in the Scriptures, that aggressive behavior tends to arouse anger, vengeance, and hostility in the person being attacked. Another certainty: though aggressive actions may initially bring compliance, the end result for the aggressor will usually be alienation and loneliness.

Passive Behavior

Passive behavior is the exact opposite of aggression. Passive people tend to be doormats, letting others walk all over them. They seldom let people know what they want or think and usually can't say no and stick to it. Passive people also have difficulty making friends and may find it impossible to accept or give a compliment. They usually avoid disagreements at all cost, saying to themselves, *He might be unhappy if I disagreed with him.*

If you find yourself doing and thinking some of the following, then portions of your everyday actions are passive and self-defeating.

1. Constantly telling yourself such things as, *She'll be disappointed if I don't do what she wants.*

2. Concerned about meeting everybody else's expectations first, no matter how much you are in need.

3. Finding that simple decisions are difficult because you want to please everyone.

4. Constantly wishing you could do certain things, yet never actually doing them.

5. Thinking, *They'll believe I'm conceited if I say something nice about myself.*

6. Wanting to meet someone, but hesitating to do so out of fear he or she might reject you.

7. Being indirect in your conversation with others.

8. Collecting a lot of anger, because you don't speak up on

a daily basis concerning your own feelings.

9. Attempting to read other people's minds, to make sure you will say what they want to hear.

10. Consistently feeling as though you have to be submissive in order to keep peace.

Assertive Behavior

Christians are told to grow up "speaking the truth in love" (Eph. 4:15). Paul also said, "Therefore, rejecting all falsity and done now with it, let everyone express the truth with his neighbor, for we are all parts of one body and members one of another" (Eph. 4:25, AMP).

Looking through a large number of recent books on assertiveness, I could not find a better definition of the term than this: *Assertive people communicate honestly.* They are positive in their relations with others, and take responsibility for themselves. Assertive persons stand up for their own rights without ignoring the rights of others.

The best example we have of the assertive life is that of Jesus. For example, He spoke His mind with His disciples in the Garden of Gethsemane after they fell asleep when He needed them most. Jesus was so full of agony that "His sweat became like great drops of blood" falling down on the ground. Returning to His closest friends, He found them asleep and asked them, "Why are you sleeping? Get up and pray so that you will not fall into temptation" (Luke 22:46, NIV). Jesus experienced a human need. He needed the concern and prayers of His friends. And He expressed His need openly and directly.

With the Pharisees, Jesus was direct and assertive. He answered their questions with honesty and candor. (For a good example, read Luke 20 in a recent version or paraphrase.) There are countless other examples of Christ's assertiveness. Passing the sycamore tree which Zaccheus had climbed into, "Jesus looked up at Zaccheus and called him by name! 'Zaccheus,' He said, 'Quick! Come down! For I am going to be a guest in your home today!' " (Luke 19:5, LB)

When Jesus called out to Peter, James, and John to follow Him and become His disciples, He did not say, "Come on you unfortunate slobs, consider yourselves lucky to follow a hotshot like Me." That would have been an aggressive statement, the kind that I've heard in similar forms in today's business world.

Nor did Jesus coax them to follow Him by beating around the bush. Can you imagine Him saying, "Do you think that you might be able to . . . er . . . that is . . . you probably wouldn't consider following Me for just a few hours, would you?"

No, Jesus was not a passive person. He was direct, yet not abusive. He took the guesswork out of communication by stating straightforwardly, "Follow me, and I will make you become fishers of men" (Mark 1:17). You see, Christ believed that people are responsible for themselves and can make their own decisions about what they will and won't do. So why beat around the bush and waste time and energy with indirect, deceitful approaches? He would ask people to be His followers in an honest, positive manner. If they refused, that was their choice. And if they accepted, they knew what they were saying yes to.

Assertiveness Is Situational

One final word about assertiveness as a principle for living. Jesus was not always assertive (Matt. 27:12-14). And it is not always desirable for you to be assertive. For instance, you want to say something directly to your boss but, based on experience, you know that you could lose your job in the process. You have already made the decision to keep your job. In that case, knowing the consequences, you might choose not to be assertive. That's OK, because you are still being responsible for your own behavior. You, ultimately, have to live with the consequences of your words and deeds.

Assertive Behaviors

In a helpful book, *Project You,** 10 types of assertive behaviors are discussed. In this chapter I want to list some of these behaviors and give you examples and offer strategies for becoming more assertive in your own life.

Express Honest Compliments

God's Word tells us to "encourage one another" (1 Thess. 5:11). Research psychologists tell us that there is nothing that can motivate people more than positive feedback. They refer to "positive thinking." If you appreciate someone or something he did, tell him. Let people know that you value even the things they "should" do, such as cooking meals, doing schoolwork, shoveling snow from the walk, buying groceries, typing a letter, and finishing a job on schedule.

But first, your compliments must be sincere and specific. If the only motive you have in mind for your kind words is flattery, forget it. People can see right through insincerity. The positive feedback you give must be true. Second, your compliments should be specific. Instead of saying to a child, "You're a good mathematician!" it's generally better to describe what you see that is good. For example, "You finished all your math problems and they're all correct; that's neat!" Now these are words a budding young third-grader can believe, especially if he has been struggling with math concepts all year.

Here are some general compliments, along with more specific ways of saying them:

GENERAL: "You're a super lover."
SPECIFIC: "I like the way you rub my back."

GENERAL: "You're fantastic."
SPECIFIC: "I like the way you express yourself."

---

*Project You, Claudine Paris and Bill Casey. Denver: Institute of Living Skills, 1976.

GENERAL: "You're a great receptionist!"
SPECIFIC: "I like the way you put people at ease."

In my own family counseling practice I have noticed time after time how a wife complains that her husband does not give her specific reasons why he loves her. Men, if you want to really build some warmth between you and your wife, give her some sincere, specific compliments. Of course, that works both ways. Wives should feel perfectly free to do the same!

If you have difficulty expressing your appreciation toward others, begin with nonverbal compliments. For example, eye contact alone compliments the person you're speaking to. Looking directly into the speaker's eyes says to that person that you value him and what he is saying. Winking at someone is another type of nonverbal positive feedback. Nodding and smiling are others forms of simple, low-risk compliments.

Since positive feedback is the most powerful human motivator, employers who are sick and tired of reminding, cajoling, and yelling at people to do their work, might try giving positive feedback to their employees. Or, if you are in a troubled relationship at home and are weary of the constant fighting and bickering, begin today giving one honest, specific compliment per day to that significant other person. Then increase the number to two per day, then three, then four—and watch what happens.

In general, accentuating the positive does several things:

1. It helps you develop into a positive, fun person to be around.

2. It helps you discover more of the positive aspects of life and decreases the chance that you will become caught up in a bitter kind of existence.

3. You become a model of kindness toward others at work, home, church, etc.

I'd like to ask you two simple thought questions:

1. Are you kinder to the people in your own family, or to strangers? Says John Gottman, in his book on couple commu-

nication: "The most consistent research finding about what is different in the communication of strangers and people married to each other is that married people are ruder to each other than they are to strangers. They interrupt their spouses more, put their spouses down more, and are less complimentary to each other."*

2. When was the last time that you actually scanned your environment for positive things? When was the last day that you looked more for positive happenings than you did for the negative?

Small Beginnings
Here are some small beginnings toward expressing honest compliments:

1. Smile at someone you don't know.
2. Give eye contact and smile at someone you care for.
3. Compliment someone for a specific behavior ("I like the way you listen to me").
4. Touch someone and smile.
5. Tell someone you appreciate his or her love, friendship, help, or support.
6. Thank someone for doing something he was "supposed to do."
7. Set a goal to give a certain number of compliments per day.

Now add your own small beginnings. What are you willing to do this next week:

8. _____

9. _____

10. _____

---

*John Gottman, *A Couple's Guide to Communication*. Champaign, Illinois: Research Press, 1976, p. 45.

Ask for What You Want

Have you ever experienced the following scene? It's Saturday night. Perhaps you are with a friend or sweetheart. You're both thinking about what you could do together for the evening. Your friend is thinking about attending a party, while you are wanting to watch a TV special. But neither of you speaks up for what he or she wants.

Instead, the first audible sound comes from your friend, "Well, what do you want to do?"

You reply, "Oh, I don't know. What do you want to do?"

Your friend mumbles something about a party that you know you don't want to go to. You mumble something about TV but quickly add that you can skip it. So you both end up aimlessly drifting off to the party. The result is that you have a miserable evening, and even become angry with your friend who has "forced you to attend the party." You've both just lost a game of "I don't know—what do you want?"

Recently I counseled with a couple about their marriage relationship. The husband, Steve, rarely asked his wife, Joy, for what he needed or wanted in their relationship. He would call from work and say vague things such as, "I just don't know what I'm going to do about this job." What he really needed from Joy was for her to just listen to his quandary at work for a moment and support him in whatever decision he came up with. Yet he never came right out and asked, "I just need you to listen to me for a few minutes."

Joy rarely knew what Steve really wanted in their relationship. As a result, Steve became more convinced that she just did not care about his needs. His silence and vagueness, coupled with Joy's resulting nonresponse, led to Steve's suicide attempt and his threats to leave home. As Steve was furiously moving his clothes and personal belongings out of the house, he finally blurted out, "It would only take three words to keep me here: those words are 'I love you.'"

This was the first direct request Steve had made of Joy in 10 years of marriage. After Joy recovered from the shock she responded quickly and directly with those three words Steve had asked for!

Each time I think of this situation I can't help but see both its humor and its tragedy. Steve had gone through 10 years of agony, largely because he did not ask for want he wanted. And when he saw Joy's willingness to respond to his requests, he was absolutely floored.

But asking for what you want does not guarantee that you'll always get it. To expect that would be to follow the thinking of a child who "wants what he wants" and "wants it now!" The point is: unless you make your needs known to other people, how will they know what you want? Try as we might, man has yet to come up with a good technique for mind reading. Yet a lot of wasted time and energy is spent trying to read each other's minds in business relationships, personal interactions, and even with casual acquaintances.

What happens when people do not express their needs to each other openly? One major pattern I see is the buildup of anger and self-pity. If we go around expecting other people to read our minds, then the next step is to begin telling ourselves, "She just doesn't care what I think" . . . "He never does anything I want" . . . "Why should I have to tell her?" At some point, our bitterness will blow up in someone's face when we present him with a whole list of injustices. The other person is initially quite shocked and confused about our feelings because he had no idea we were thinking these things! The self-pity we then talk ourselves into creates an attitude that we are not responsible for ourselves. But this idea is simply false.

Again, here are some suggestions for getting started with asking for what you want.

1. Ask for an opinion.
2. Ask for a clarification of what someone says.
3. Ask for a favor.
4. Ask for a behavior change (e.g., "Could you please speak more loudly?").
5. Begin some sentences with phrases such as, "Would you

please . . ." "I would appreciate your saying . . ." "I need. . . ."

SOME POINTS TO REMEMBER:

1. People have the right to refuse your requests.

2. Requests are not demands. Often you can't make a person do anything unless you use physical force.

3. Make your requests in a direct, loving manner.

4. Do not ask for what you want when you are extremely angry. Wait until you've cooled down.

State Honest Disagreements with Ease

Stating disagreements "with ease" is tough for most of us. Let's take a look at how we can approach this goal.

If you are a human being with values of your own there are times when you disagree with what other people say. Sometimes you choose to remain silent, but other times you want to speak out for the values you hold, especially if your silence could be interpreted as compliance or agreement with an opinion that is completely contrary to what you hold sacred.

Can you imagine what this world would be like if no one ever openly disagreed with anyone else? Christianity would never have been founded; the United States would not be a reality; and instead of hopping aboard a jet to Calgary, Canada next month I'd be walking, starting last January!

In disagreeing wth someone else we often think, *Perhaps he won't like me anymore, and I don't want that to happen.* What this attitude fails to consider is that we could be increasing the risk of that person not liking or respecting us if we do *not* speak up for what we believe in.

I see children and adolescents who simply do not respect their parents because Mom and Dad seldom, if ever, state their opinions directly. Children desperately need parents to share their own values, philosophies, and opinions about life. Our little ones must have adult models so they can form a basis and "home ground" for living their own lives.

Certainly there comes a time when children choose their own values and ideas, but they cannot do a very good job of this in the vacuum of permissiveness. We need to share our values with our kids and act on them, so they can actually see what "believing in God" and "trusting each other" look like.

Some Principles for Disagreeing

Here are some guidelines to consider when you choose to openly disagree with someone:

1. STICK TO THE ISSUE. Many disagreements develop into all-out battles because of "kitchen-sinking." These people drag everything into the conversation except the kitchen sink. The discussion starts on one issue and before there is a chance to explore that issue, one person drags in other disagreements that usually are not even related. When "kitchen-sinking" occurs, a simple, "I think we're getting off the track" may be all that is needed.

2. DON'T ATTACK THE OTHER PERSON. Many problems arise when we stop talking about the issue and begin to attack the other person. If you have difficulty with this, write down the following two verses on a note card, carry the card around with you, and read it several times a day: "Self-control means controlling the tongue! A quick retort can ruin everything" (Prov. 13:3, LB). "A good man thinks before he speaks; the evil man pours out his evil words without a thought" (Prov. 15:28, LB).

3. DISAGREE FIRST ON SMALL MATTERS, IN LOW-RISK RELATIONSHIPS. By doing this you'll get a feel for what it's like for you to disagree with someone. You'll discover the kinds of tactics people use to get you off the track. For example, at a social gathering a few days ago, I was seated next to a person from out of state. He immediately began complaining about the rotten weather we were having in our city, how smoggy it was, and how unfriendly the people were. This was a person I would probably never see again. So he represented a low-risk relationship. He continued, "This city is cold, smoggy, and unfriendly. There is no way I'd live here."

I responded by saying, "I don't know what cities you've been in. I've really experienced Denver as having a comfortable, moderate climate with lots of warm, sunny days."

He added, "Well the people here are really cold and ruthless."

I replied, "My experience has been different from yours on that score also. I've had more close friends here than in any other community I've lived."

When I disagreed I did not critize him for his attitude. I stated my opinion and the specific reasons I had for forming my opinion. I did not attempt to reform him. I merely asserted my point of view. This illustrates two more principles:

4. STATE YOUR OPINION AND THE SPECIFIC REASONS FOR FORMING YOUR OPINION.

5. DO NOT ATTEMPT TO REFORM THE OTHER PERSON.

Once you are able to disagree about small unimportant matters in low-risk relationships, move on to issues of greater importance for you. Some of these "heavier" topics might be how to raise children, politics, religion, the future of the American family, women's liberation, and maybe which pro team will win the division title.

The next step is to speak out about unimportant issues with persons you know more intimately. Finally, you can ease into important issues with the people you find are the most difficult to disagree with.

6. LEARN HOW TO SAY, "I WAS WRONG." If, in the middle of a disagreement, you put somebody down or if you later realize that your adamantly held position was incorrect, admit your mistake. You might say, "I'm sorry for my error" or "I think your evidence is more convincing than mine." The Book of Proverbs speaks to this principle from several angles: "The intelligent man is always open to new ideas. In fact, he looks for them" (Prov. 18:15, LB). "The selfish man quarrels against every sound principle of conduct by demanding his own way" (Prov. 18:1, LB).

7. AGREE TO DISAGREE. There are times when people close to you will simply disagree with your opinion. At that point, you can "agree to disagree" instead of getting locked into a winlose type of battle. We just can't agree with each other on

every subject. Accept that fact and you'll save yourself much misery in life.

Small Beginnings

1. Play "devil's advocate" in a small group.

2. When someone states an opinion you disagree with slightly, say so.

3. When someone misinterprets something you said, tell him so.

4. If a friend expresses a different opinion on a program or a book, state your opinion.

Be Able to Say No

Working at a university a few years back I had been under constant pressure to serve on numerous committees, task forces, and pilot groups. No matter what these little groups are called they mean two things: extra work and extra time. I could handle a few committees but when I became too involved in too many of them, I lost sight of my mission as a university professor: that of teaching and other scholarly activity. I decided I was serving on enough of these "problem-solving" groups and that I would form a policy of saying no to any further requests for committee work.

I immediately called several offices that might make such requests and stated the following: "I would like your office to know in advance that I will not be able to take on any more committee assignments for this academic year. So if you are thinking about me for such an assignment, you should consider an alternative. I am already serving on several committees and feel I can only do justice to their activities if I remain at my present work load." So I warned these offices in advance that I would be saying no to their requests.

Lucky me! About three days later I received a call from one of the offices I had warned in advance. The receptionist began with flattery: "We have a committee assignment for you that fits you like a glove. We could think of no other person to call who would have the expertise which you can bring to this policy-making group. And the Dean (she's putting some weight behind this) would be very pleased if you would take it."

My reply went something like, "I'm very flattered (took a knot of wind out of her sails) that you and the Dean think so highly of my skills, but as I stated to you three days ago over the telephone I simply cannot take any more assignments." The conversation continued:

RECEPTIONIST: "This appointment might really help you in terms of promotion," etc.

ME: "The Dean has already stated to me that he is most pleased with my work as a teacher and scholar. In order to continue as a productive faculty member I simply cannot spread myself too thin. If I do I'll not do any of my tasks very well."

RECEPTIONIST (*she's not ready to give up just yet*): "We just can't think of anyone else who will fill the bill. We would really benefit from your abilities."

ME: "Again I truly appreciate your dilemma and your confidence in me, but in order to continue as a productive faculty member I simply must limit my committee assignments at this time. Tell the Dean that I really appreciate his thinking of me and that I know how difficult it is to find committee members, but that I cannot take the position."

RECEPTIONIST (*one last effort*): "OK, I'll tell the Dean!"

ME: "Thank you" (*in a friendly tone*).

In this interchange I followed several guidelines which are important in saying no.

1. WHEN POSSIBLE, WARN PEOPLE IN ADVANCE THAT YOU ARE GOING TO SAY NO. This prepares them for your eventual action. It also gives you the opportunity to begin to say your no in a less anxiety-producing situation. It tends to discourage people from asking you for the favor or request. Advance warning also cuts down the hope which the other person has of getting what he wants. So he may be less persistent.

2. USE THE "BROKEN RECORD." Each time the receptionist utilized a different strategy to convince me, I essentially re-

peated in similar words what my position was. This kept me on target. I did not get sidetracked. When she said, "*We* just can't think of anyone else," I merely reiterated that I could not accept the position and why. After three "broken records" she took my no for an answer. Some people have to hear your no only once, but others need to hear it five or six times before they take you seriously. The point is to keep repeating it and don't get sidetracked into other issues.

3. VALIDATE THE REQUESTER'S DILEMMA. By saying, "I truly appreciate your dilemma" and "I know how difficult it is to find committee members," I was validating the feelings the receptionist had about her task. I was caring enough to at least communicate to her that I was listening and appreciated her plight. I genuinely empathized with her. Yet this did not mean I was obligated to say yes.

Why do I believe that saying no is such an important thing to be able to do? Because some of the world's greatest martyrs are persons who *can't* say no. These people often complain that others take advantage of them or that they never have time for themselves or their families. Yet they miss the fact that they are responsible for their own lives and that it is their perfect right to say no.

Another reason why this assertive skill is so important is that continued favors tend to become rights. If I hadn't at some point stood my ground on the committee work, various offices around the university would have assumed that I'd say yes to all requests. "Schmidt will do it; he never says no to anything," would have been heard when the administrators were putting together some new task force. And once it's assumed that you will behave in a particular way, it's twice as difficult to try to change people's minds.

Saying no at the time may be tough. It's too easy to tell yourself, *Oh, it's just not worth the hassle; I'll do it. Then no one will be upset with me. Besides, a good person must do favors for others.* Let's take a look at these words for a moment. First, you say it's just not worth the hassle. But what kind of hassles do you run into after you've said yes to something that you dread doing? Don't you have just as many, if not more hassles then? And usually the thing you've said yes to lasts longer than a simple no would have taken.

How many times have you said yes to a request you wanted to say no to, and later, had to turn it down anyway? And usually you had to back out just before you were to perform the favor. How pleased do you think that other person was at that point? Or perhaps you went along with the request and were either extremely unenthusiastic or did a poor job. How do you think the other individual felt about that kind of response?

Finally, take the phrase, *A good person must do favors for others*. True, if I am to have some close relationships I will need to do favors for others. However, if I don't set priorities for my time and energy by saying yes to some things and no to others, then I will have relinquished control of my life. By saying yes to all demands from the outside, without making my own decisions about those demands, I have no plan for my own living. Can I be a good person if I say yes to so many outside demands that I end up neglecting my job, my family, my marriage, and my relationship with God? How can I expect my children to become responsible adults, able to make value judgments and say no to immoral acts, if they see me completely controlled by the external world?

Offer Alternatives

In my exchange with the Dean's office I did not offer any alternative names that the receptionist might call and ask to be on the committee. I value my friendships with my colleagues too much for that! However, this can sometimes be a further step to take when saying no to someone. For example, your spouse has just asked you to talk with her. But you are looking forward to a short, refreshing nap at this time. You had a very demanding day at the office and really need a breather. You might say something like, "I can tell from the sound of your voice that whatever you want to talk about is really important. But I've had a really demanding day and I'd like just 10 minutes to relax and get my thoughts together. I'll be in a lot better shape to talk in just a few minutes." In this way you don't put your spouse off indefinitely. Instead, you offer an alternative time to talk 10 minutes from now. And both of your rights as individuals have been honored.

Let's look at some other examples, along with possible responses that offer alternatives:

SALLY (*to a girl friend*): "Would you like to go shopping tonight?"

MARY: "No, Sally, I don't care to go out tonight. How about going on Friday night?"

In this way Mary is saying to Sally, "Look, I value our friendship enough to want to go out with you somewhere soon, but tonight I just don't care to go anywhere."

Keep in Touch with Friends
Working as a professor had become too demanding. There were many other activities besides teaching which occupied my time. Soon it became easy to isolate myself in my work and not have enough time for coffee breaks, chitchats with colleagues, or lunch. I was busily struggling for a promotion through publications, teaching, serving on several dissertation committees, and heading task forces, plus a few other things. Then one morning I saw this quote in the newspaper:

"To let friendship die away by negligence and silence is certainly not wise. It is voluntary to throw away one of the greatest comforts of this weary pilgrimage" (Johnson).

These words hit home like a jackhammer! I decided to do two things:

1. I would have lunch with my colleagues at least twice a week. This meant if I were to ask someone for lunch and he turned me down I would ask another person and another until I had two luncheon engagements arranged for that week.

2. I would organize an informal "feelings" meeting among interested faculty on a weekly basis. This meant getting to-

gether for about an hour over coffee to discuss our concerns and celebrations for that week.

Next day I set up my two luncheons for the week. And after night class that evening I entered a professor's office where several of my collegues were gathered. Each person in the room looked tired and upset. I said, "You people look as worn out as I feel." There were several affirmative sighs. I suggested the weekly "feelings" gathering and everyone enthusiastically agreed to try it. This began a series of relief-giving, sharing times together.

I remembered that one of my students had said, "Friendships are not bookkeeping arrangements. If you want to spend some time with a friend, just do it. Don't worry about whether that person contacted you last or whether it's your turn or not." She was right. When I began to express my feelings of isolation with other faculty members they said they felt the same way. Several admitted that they were sitting around waiting for others to make the initial contact or that they felt it was someone else's turn to initiate contact. Meanwhile, most of us were miserable and secluded from each other, keeping our books: "Let's see—I called him last. Now it's his turn to ask me for coffee."

Keeping in touch with friends helps you receive the "strokes," "warm fuzzies," and the fun times that you need in order to function. Being with a friend also helps when you're down. A friend a day keeps depression away. And people are usually pleased when you contact them. Paul summed it up nicely: "For the Holy Spirit, God's gift, does not want you to be afraid of people, but to be wise and strong, and to love them and enjoy being with them" (2 Tim. 1:7, LB).

So if you're sitting there wanting to be with someone you like, call that friend, now. If the person is not home, don't give up. Call again in an hour. If he or she has plans and can't be with you when you'd like, set up an alternative time when you can get together.

Avoid saying such things to yourself as, *They refused my dinner invitation because I'm a terrible host,* or *He didn't call me, so he doesn't like me*. More often than not these thoughts are simply erroneous. Look at the facts. Are you a terrible host? Who has told you this? How many have told you just the opposite? Perhaps he didn't call you because he's been out of town, or busy with work. Give him a break. Call him. Give yourself and him some comfort, some fun, and some enjoyment. Keep in touch with friends. They're God's gifts.

10
Perfectionism

Mark hurled his hammer across the room. It crashed into the utility room door, leaving a telltale crater-like indentation. Mark's violent temper had come to the fore once again.

The crash brought his wife Cheri, downstairs immediately to check out what had happened. As Mark somewhat sheepishly explained, Cheri's eyes revealed escalating feelings of anger and disgust. She read Mark the riot act and stormed back upstairs, mumbling something about now having *one more* child in the house.

What had led up to all this? First, you need to know that for Mark nothing can be "average," "above average," "quite good," or "well done." Whatever Mark does must be perfect. This is all-or-nothing thinking. In fact, he and I often joked about the fact that for him there were "no grays," only "blacks and whites."

Mark had been working on a wooden cabinet that morning. It was the first cabinet he had ever tried to make, but he was expecting to make *no* mistakes, even though he was using plywood for parts of the cabinet. He had just slightly split one of the ends on a piece of wood when he heaved his hammer across the room.

Later I talked with Mark about his automatic thoughts. He

said they went something like this: *Because I cracked this piece of plywood, I'll never learn to make cabinets. I'm a worthless, stupid idiot! I can't do anything right! I may as well give up working with my hands. And I thought I was good at this! I'm living in a fantasy world! I give up!*

One of the strategies I suggested for Mark was to list the advantages and disadvantages of perfectionistic thinking. Here's what he came up with:

ADVANTAGES

1. I'll do exceptional work or at least I *might* do exceptional work.
2. Whatever I attempt, I'll try very hard to do well at it.

DISADVANTAGES

1. I'll be eternally frustrated.
2. I'll continue to "blow up" a lot.
3. I'll do my wood-working projects so slowly that I'll be unlikely to make a profit on what I sell.
4. Because of my frustration I'll continue to be a grouch around the house.
5. It's likely that my blood pressure will continue to rise, increasing my risk of heart disease or a stroke.
6. Since I can never be perfect I'll continue to be depressed.
7. All this perfectionism keeps me from trying out any suggestions my therapist is giving me. I don't try out any new things that might help me grow as a person or just enjoy myself.

Facing Your Fear

When I finished my Ph.D. in 1972 I vowed that I would never communicate on paper again. The pick-apart, scrutinizing process of writing a dissertation had killed any desire I previously had for writing. In fact, I don't recall ever looking at my dissertation since. I'd figured that any journal article or book I wrote as a professor at Denver University would have to be even more "perfect" than my doctoral thesis.

But the pressure was on. In order to gain a higher rank and tenure at the university I would have to have something published. Now I had to face my fear. What fear? I was afraid someone would criticize what I had written. Then what? Well, if an editor criticized my work, then I'd have to rewrite it. And if I had to rewrite I would have to spend many hours on it. And what if I *never* pleased the editors? Well, that would prove I'm not a worthy faculty member and certainly not a scholar. Then what? Well, if I'm not a scholar then maybe I'm not bright enough to be teaching in my field.

Wait a minute! Do you see how I had talked myself into a terminal state of paralysis? As long as I never typed anything I'd never have to face my fear. Or if I could just work slowly enough or procrastinate enough, nothing would ever be submitted to an editor. If nothing were submitted, I'd never be rejected.

Then a godsend occurred. The voice on the other end of a long-distance call was from Champaign, Illinois. It was Ann Wendel, Senior Editor for Research Press. She had heard me speak at a convention in New Orleans and liked what I said. She wanted a couple of chapters and outline for a book on self-modification procedures. She gave me a deadline. Now it was either put up or shut up. Funny how God puts me in frightening situations every now and then so that I have a chance to grow. I was pleased, flattered, and scared. But now there was no time to get everything perfect. Ann wanted a "rough draft" quickly. I sat at the typewriter in our barren basement and the words began to flow. In four days I had a "rough draft," submitted the chapters to a few colleagues for critique, made some corrections, and sent them to Research Press.

What would you guess were my thoughts, my expectations? You're right! I fully expected Ann to apologetically but firmly suggest that I stick to conventions. Or at best I figured that the chapters would be returned saturated with red marks, criticisms, and complete rewrite suggestions. Much to my surprise Ann called back stating that she liked what I had written and would be sending a contract in a few weeks. And could I finish the remaining nine chapters in the next six months? Facing my fear had given me a piece of new information about writing. A Gail Sheely or Charles Swindoll I'm not. But maybe I've got something that can be communicated in writing. Something that can help others.

I've learned that most of my fears, when faced, are far less threatening than what I had allowed my mind to imagine. It's also interesting how God places me in situations that used to absolutely terrify me. Why? Not because I had actually experienced them, but because I had built up all kinds of erroneous automatic thoughts concerning terrible things that would happen if I got into these situations. And I added further pressure on myself by insisting that I do them all perfectly the first time.

The "Then-What" Approach

Some time ago a young man came to me quite depressed and anxious. He was teaching at a college. Ed would spend hours and hours preparing for lectures, attempting to make them so flawless that no one could possibly criticize what he was saying. Another goal of Ed's was to construct his lectures so precisely that students would have no questions about what he was saying. Can you imagine the number of hours it would take to prepare just one such lecture? And can you imagine the amount of pressure Ed felt as he stood before his students?

I asked Ed, among other things, to employ the "Then-What" approach. In this approach you keep asking yourself questions such as, "If this happens, then what?" "If this thought were true, why would it upset me?" You keep asking yourself these questions until you uncover all the silent assumptions that underly your automatic thoughts. Here's what Ed came up with:

AUTOMATIC THOUGHTS

1. My lecture was less than perfect.
   THEN WHAT?

2. My students will notice all the flaws and the unclear parts.
   THEN WHAT?

3. They'll feel that I don't give a rip about what I'm doing.
   THEN WHAT?

4. Then I'll be letting them down.
   THEN WHAT?

5. I'll get very low student evaluations.
   THEN WHAT?

ALTERNATIVE THOUGHTS

1. This is all-or-nothing thinking. The lecture must have been fairly decent. Several made favorable comments.

2. Sure, they probably will notice some flaws, but they'll consider the lecture was pretty good.

3. This is mind reading. I don't *know* they will think this. Even if they did, it wouldn't be the end of the world. Besides I do care a lot, probably too much, about how I'm doing.

4. More all-or-nothing thinking. I can't always please everyone. They seem to like most of my lectures. If they're disappointed today, they'll live through it.

5. This is emotional reasoning and mind reading. I'm acting like a fortune-teller. I can't predict the future. I may get average or above average student evaluations, but low or very low isn't likely.

6. That would completely ruin my academic career as a faculty member.
THEN WHAT?

7. This would mean that I'm not the kind of teacher I'm supposed to be.
THEN WHAT?

8. People will be angry with me. I'll be a failure.
THEN WHAT?

9. Then I would be snubbed, ignored, and left completely alone.
AND THEN WHAT?

10. If I'm alone, I'll be miserable for the rest of my life.

6. All-or-nothing thinking. Again I'm acting like a fortune-teller. Other people goof up and it doesn't ruin their careers. Why can't I mess up sometimes?

7. This is a should statement. How good am I supposed to be anyway? Who says I have to be perfect? Does God?

8. Mind reading. All-or-nothing thinking. How do I know people will be angry with me? And what if they are? That's really their problem. I can't always please everyone. This thought makes me tense, rigid, and constricted. If I fail as a professor it doesn't make *me* a failure.

9. I'm acting like a fortune-teller again! Not everyone will snub me or ignore me.

10. I'm disqualifying my positive data. I've had really happy times alone. How do I know I'll be miserable forever? My misery comes from perfectionistic standards, not because I'll probably be alone.

Can you see how Ed continued to peel off layer after layer until he had revealed the deepest origin of his panic? In this way we uncovered the basis of his perfectionism. One silent assumption that became obvious was, *One mistake and my career will be ended.* Another misbelief sounded something like, *People require that I be perfect. If I'm not they will ostracize and snub me.* Once Ed actually had written out his entire thinking process, he began to see all the mental distortions and unrealistic thoughts he was laying on himself. Finally he got to the bottom line: *What's the worst thing that could happen?* Ed admitted that the worst thing probably never would happen, but that he was acting as if it already had.

You might ask, what if Ed *had* received poor evaluations from his students? First, this is unlikely since perfectionists tend to work so hard that complete failure is highly unlikely. Second, let's say that he had received very low evaluations. Then he could evaluate why this had happened. He could tape a lecture and have a colleague, friend, or his wife listen to it. These people could offer their opinions as to what Ed might improve on. Or he could consider another career. That might be tough. It would be discouraging, but it would not have to lead to his being "miserable forever."

Of course, Ed wasn't completely convinced even after this "Then what?" exercise. But when his student evaluations came back they were excellent! I find this so often happens with perfectionists. In the end they usually do much better than they ever expected. But if you are a perfectionist, you will have to confront the bogeyman, whoever he is. It will be tough. It will be scary. But it will be less terrifying if you write down your automatic thoughts and begin asking yourself, "What am I afraid of?" and "What's the worst thing that could happen?"

The Goal or the Process?

Christ knew what would happen to Him. He would be crushed, rejected, and killed by His own people. What would have happened to His life if He had continually worried about its end? He might have run scared all His life. Jesus might have remained in seclusion; He might have lived a pretty defensive life. Instead, Jesus focused on what was going on presently. He related to people in their moments of need. Sure, there were times when He contemplated His demise. But the way He responded as a fully functioning person in the "now" shows that His principle thoughts were not about His death.

Here's another way to illustrate my point. Glenwood Canyon near Glenwood Springs, Colorado, is a beautiful drive. The Colorado River flows through dark, rugged walls that reach 500 feet or more above. At different times of the day the huge rock formations take on various hues and tones of purple, red, blue-gray, and rust as the sun shines through at various angles. There are two ways to drive through the canyon. One is to get behind a semitruck and become frustrated, because you're thinking about the goal of reaching Glenwood Springs on the west side of the canyon. Your fists grip the steering wheel tightly and you constantly try to peer around the semi to see if you have a chance to zoom around it before oncoming traffic nails you. Your heart beats faster. You're annoyed by the kids' questions concerning how deep the river is and your wife's chattering about the beauty of the canyon. Your blood pressure rises. By the time you get through the canyon a half hour later you are absolutely exhausted from frustration, anger, and tension. Perhaps you've even said a few choice nasty words to your wife and kids. But you've reached your goal, Glenwood Springs! And you're still behind that truck.

Ah, but there's a second way to drive through the canyon. It begins the same way. You get behind a semitruck. (Note: you always get behind a semitruck while driving through Glenwood Canyon.) But this time instead of becoming hysterical over the big truck, you calmly stay farther behind it, and drink in the picturesque canyon. You respond to your wife's comments about the elegance of the gorge. You attempt to answer your children's questions. About 30 minutes later you've reached Glenwood Springs, still behind the same semi, but relaxed and at peace. Why? You've focused on the process of going through the canyon instead of on the goal on the other side.

Focusing on the process is a good way of dealing with perfectionism. Instead of continually looking ahead toward your utopian goals, enjoy the present process of getting there. In writing this book, whenever I think of 12 completed, perfect chapters, I get nervous and feel overwhelmed. But if I can concentrate on enjoying the present chapter and what I am sharing in the "now," my anxiety level drops. I can be more open to use the creativity God has given me. I am less constricted, more free to develop ideas.

How could you set up a process orientation if you're trying to do well in school? Instead of constantly worrying about that "A" at the end you can: (1) attend your classes; (2) listen and take notes; (3) keep current with your assignments; (4) attempt to enjoy what you're reading; (5) review your notes periodically. In this way, you are focusing on the process leading toward the goal of getting an "A." The point is, constant worry about whether or not you will get an "A" won't help you center your attention on the steps that lead to your goal.

Challenge Your All-or-Nothing Thinking

How many things can actually be broken down into all-or-nothing categories? The old black-and-white philosophy is part of the disease of perfectionism. Is anything in this world perfect? Is your carpet completely clean? Or is there always some dirt on it, even after you vacuum it for the third time in a row? Is what I have written perfect? Is it perfectly effective? Or just partially effective? Is anyone you know perfectly together at all times? Is your favorite song without flaw? What about your favorite singer? Is her voice without blemish?

And what about the perfectionism we get into as part of our faith? We've already discussed some of this in chapter 8, on guilt. If God had expected us to be perfect He would have never sent Christ to forgive us for our misdeeds. Yet we think we're smarter than God when we try to do everything just right. Now there's nothing wrong with trying to do things well. But if we get into all-or-nothing efforts and expect ourselves to win them all, we are playing God and really saying we need no one but ourselves. Even the great Apostle Paul admitted that he had flaws. He wrote, "It is I who am carnal, and have sold my soul to sin. In practice, what happens? My own behavior baffles me. For I find myself not doing what I really want to do but doing what I really loath. . . . And, indeed, I know from experience that the carnal side of my being can scarcely be called the home of good! I often find that I have the will to do good, but not the power. That is, I don't accomplish the good I set out to do, and the evil I don't really want to do I find I am always doing" (Rom. 7:14-15, 18-19, PH).

Are you going to compare yourself to Paul? Are you going to shoot for the absurdity of being a better Christian than Paul? Good grief! He was the giant of Christianity! He wrote 13 or maybe 14 letters in the New Testament. Even Paul didn't espouse the all-or-nothing thinking we may get into. He didn't say, "Either you live a perfect life or you're lost." Do you see that anywhere in his epistles? You've got it—nowhere!

You say, "Wait a minute, little unknown author! What about absolutes? Certainly there are some in Christianity. What about, "Unless one is born again he cannot see the kingdom of God"?

You know, you're right. There are absolutes in Christianity. And I suppose we could stand around arguing about whether some statements are absolutes or not. But here's one that is sure: There is only one way to God, according to Scripture, and that is through His Son, Jesus Christ. I can remember reading through the 27 volumes that Karl Barth had written. Barth was a neoorthodox theologian. We don't agree with much of what he wrote. But he did write on every conceivable subject related to Christian theology before he died. He was a genius. Someone estimated he had an IQ of 200. Near the end of his 27th volume he wrote, "In several years and 27 volumes of theology I have come to one absolute truth. . . . 'Jesus loves me, this I know, for the Bible tells me so.' "

Those words broke through to the innermost recesses of my mind. They have been emblazoned on my heart. So why do we waste our time and energy trying to come up with so many other black-and-white solutions and goals? Beats me. I agree, either one is a Christian or he is not. And, as C. S. Lewis indicates in *Mere Christianity*, either Christ was a crazy lunatic who had delusions that He was the Son of God or He really was, and *is*. There's no middle ground on that one. But in so many other areas the black-and-white philosophy just doesn't apply. For example:

ALL-OR-NOTHING THINKING	REALISTIC THINKING
1. I'm a complete failure.	1. I've succeeded at some things and failed at others. So join the human race. Does God think I'm a failure? Hardly. Would He bother to die for me if I were worthless?
2. I'm too old.	2. Too old for what? Too old to have a good time? No. Too old for sex? No. Too old to learn? No. Too old to love? No. Too old to enjoy music? No. So what am I too old for?
3. People don't like me.	3. I've never heard anyone say that. I have several friends who call me each week. They wouldn't call if they hated me. I was asked at church to serve as a deacon. Someone must like me.

4. I can't get over this habit. Therefore, I am not a Christian. I must be lost.

4. Where does it say in Scripture that I must break all my bad habits in order to be saved? I'll enlist God's help to change it. I'll depend on Him to help me decrease and stop the habit.

So how are you helped by claiming to be perfect, or desperately pushing yourself to be perfect? What are the advantages of being a perfectionist? What are the disadvantages? Does it actually help you reach your goals? What does it do for your self-esteem? What does it do for others? Does it help you become a better servant of God? Does perfectionism help you in your relationships with others? Does it decrease your anxiety? What does it do for depression? Does it make you more understanding toward others? What does perfectionism do for your frustration level? For your feelings of guilt? Are people either all good or all bad? Is a room either all clean or all dirty? Is a pastor's sermon perfect, or can it be worthwhile in some ways and not so helpful in other ways? Can you be less than an absolutely competent parent? Can you be aver age at anything? Do you always have a choice?

11
Anger and Resentment

Is it all right to feel angry? Should I ever express anger? In what way? What does "Do not let the sun go down on your anger" mean? (Eph. 4:26) Is a Christian supposed to inhibit his angry feelings? If not, what kind of anger can a believer express? Can I express anger toward God? Won't He blow me away if I do? Can't I carry anger too far? What's appropriate to express? How controlled should I be when I express anger?

Of all the emotions, expressing anger or just feeling angry may be the toughest for a Christian. Jesus told us to turn the other cheek (Matt. 5:39). Yet we also read that twice He became so angry that He overturned tables and threw things around in the temple (John 2:13-17; Matt. 21:12-13). We're also told to "Be angry and yet do not sin" (Eph. 4:26). What does all this mean? How does it fit together?

Are You an Angry Person?
I've heard many people ask, "Am I an angry person? Do I get too angry?"

If most of the following situations would arouse a lot of anger in you, then you are probably allowing anger to consume you:

1. You buy a toy for your son, put the batteries in—and it doesn't work.

2. You are overcharged by a garage mechanic who has you over a barrel.

3. In a hurry to get somewhere, you rip a good sport coat on a sharp object.

4. You lend someone a book and he fails to return it.

5. You are at a meeting where someone continues to try to hog the limelight, even though she's wasting time.

6. Someone teases you.

7. You are criticized for something which you don't believe is your fault.

8. Your car gets stuck in the snow or mud.

9. You talk to someone and he doesn't answer you.

10. Someone in the car behind you blares his horn and gives you an obscene gesture.

11. Your spouse or a friend complains about something you forgot to do.

12. You are on the phone, trying to clear up a big mistake on your phone bill and you have just been referred to the fourth person.

13. Someone is talking as if he were an expert on something he knows little about.

14. Someone makes a mistake and blames it on you.

15. The pastor makes a statement from the pulpit that you disagree with.

Now that you know more about how much anger you have, let's see what causes anger and what you can do about it.

What Causes Anger?

Your child runs out into the street between two parked cars. You scream at her as visions of a crumpled little body race through your mind. But nothing happens, fortunately, for no cars were coming. You jerk her back to the curb, yelling and spanking.

Why this kind of rage? Just a few moments before you were joking with her, hugging her. Fear, that's why. You saw potential disaster and your body reacted with a fear response. Your pupils dilated, sugar output increased. Your blood pressure and heart rate also increased. Adrenalin flowed more rapidly. Your entire body prepared itself for the worst. It is interesting that these same internal reactions occur when we get angry. For fear often begets anger.

Hurt is another emotion that can be expressed in the form of anger. Let's say you've just been criticized for a mistake that you already are painfully aware of. Most likely the first emotion you feel is hurt. But your defenses go up. "That creep isn't going to get to me. I've got to defend myself." You attack back in order to preserve your worthiness. So, instead of the "creep" knowing he has offended you or cut you, he sees your anger and in turn he administers a counterattack. And you get hurt again.

Both fear and hurt often lead to anger. But there's an alternate way to express this secondary feeling. You can try to express your hurt and fear. With your daughter you might yell, "Don't ever run out in the street like that! I was scared to death you might be hit by a car!"

Or to the person who offended you, "I'm already painfully aware of what you are saying."

These statements give a different message from, "You careless kid. Can't you ever pay attention to what I've told you?" Or, to the "creep," "*You* never make mistakes, huh?"

Injustice can also provoke anger. Abraham Lincoln was provoked to anger when he first observed the slave market. As he watched the atrocity he said, "Someday I'm going to hit this problem and I'm going to hit it hard!" Many people have done constructive deeds as a result of anger toward injustice.

Frustration is still another source of anger. Frustration usually involves some goal that has been blocked from your attainment. One humorous example of this is a TV commercial about a book that solves the Rubik's Cube. (The goal is to match up each side of the cube with the identical color through a series of rotating movements of the sides of the cube.) The ad shows people becoming so frustrated over not being able to solve the puzzle that they throw tantrums, run over the Cube with a steamroller, and throw it out the window of a car while no one is watching.

A more serious frustration might come if your goal is to find a mate and Mr. or Miss Right simply is nowhere to be found. Your frustration may then turn into anger and disillusionment. You may start saying to yourself, "All women are alike." Or, "All men want the same thing." You could develop a lot of bitterness and resentment toward all members of the opposite sex and completely sabotage your efforts to find a spouse because of a chip on your shoulder.

What Does Scripture Say about Anger?

Several Greek words are used for anger in the New Testament. Many people think that the Bible contradicts itself because sometimes we are taught not to be angry (Col. 3:8, e.g.) and elsewhere we are admonished to "be angry and sin not" (Eph. 4:26, kjv). The reason for this is that in different passages distinct Greek words are used. Thus, certain kinds of anger are less desirable than others.

For example, one Greek word for anger is *thumos*. *Thumos* is an agitated condition of the feelings, an outburst of wrath from inward indignation. This type of anger blazes up into a sudden explosion. *Thumos* is mentioned 20 times in passages such as Galatians 5:20. We are to control this type of anger.

A second form of anger in the Greek is *orge*. *Orge* suggests a more settled or abiding condition of mind, frequently with a view of taking revenge. *Orge* is less sudden in its rise than *thumos*, but more lasting in its nature. This is the most common form of anger mentioned in the New Testament. It is used 45 times. According to H. Norman Wright there are only two places where this word is used and revenge is not included in its meaning. In Ephesians 4:26 we are told not to "let the sun go down on your anger." And Mark (3:5) records Jesus as having looked upon the Pharisees "with anger." In these two verses the word means an abiding and sealed habit of the mind which is aroused under certain conditions against evil and injustice. This is the type of anger that Christians are encouraged to have—an anger that includes no revenge.*

So the Apostle Paul tells us to "be angry and sin not." Thus, the Scriptures not only permit anger but on some occasions demand it. In Phillips' paraphrase the prior verse says, "Finish, then, with lying and tell your neighbor the truth. For we are not separate units but intimately related to each other in Christ." Then, in verse 26, "If you are angry, be sure that it is not out of wounded pride or bad temper." So how do we do this? How do we, while angry, tell our neighbor the truth and yet not do it out of hurt pride or in a bad temper? We've covered some of this ground already in chapter 9. But according to our little Greek word study, our anger should not include revenge. It should not be expressed in the form of a counterattack. It should not be vented in heated, unrestrained passion. Our minds should be in control of our emotions so that our ability to reason is not lost. So how do we use our minds and reason in our anger? Let's take a look.

The Mind and Anger

Remember the distortions we discussed in chapter 4? Such distortions are often used in adding fuel to our *thumos* anger. *Labeling* is a chief culprit in this regard. When you categorize someone as "a jerk" or "a bum" or "irresponsible" or "worthless," you see him in a totally negative way. When you do this you completely write him off in your mind. You go on finding other examples of how this person is "irresponsible" or how your husband is "a jerk." The more you look for evidence the more you find it and the more anger you store up. Of course, in this process you lead yourself into another distortion in your thinking, *mental filter*.

This further distortion is *disqualifying the positive*. You ignore or discount that other person's good points. You will *not* give yourself a chance to overcome your anger. You keep

---

*H. Norman Wright, *An Answer to Anger and Frustration*. Irvine, California: Harvest House, 1977, pp. 13-14.

feeding the anger with your "mental filter" attitude. Of course, all this labeling and disqualifying the positive along with mental filter cause you to respond like a real turkey. And pretty soon that other person is treating you like a true "jerk" and then you have even more evidence of how awful she is.

Wait a minute! How do you get out of this cycle? One way is to *list the advantages and disadvantages of thinking the way you are*. How will thinking your husband is a complete loser help you build that relationship? Will it help your husband feel better about himself? Is it likely to help him in his relationship with God? Will it help him in his role as a husband? Will your "mental filter" attitude send him off to work in good spirits?

A second strategy is to *restate what you're saying to yourself: She may be reacting irresponsibly at this moment and I don't like it. But that doesn't make my roommate irresponsible in every way. I can't reduce her to one category—irresponsible! Or I would define a jerk as someone who is absolutely mindless. Bill is in no way "absolutely mindless." At this moment he may be a little scatterbrained, but he also is quite astute in many situations*

These two alternate ways of thinking are likely to help you come to conclusions that are more in line with the truth.

Another distortion we can get into rather easily is *mind reading*. Here you invent interpretations and motives that explain why someone did something you didn't like. Some examples:

"She didn't call me because she dislikes me."

"He was angry with me because he thinks I'm really stupid."

"My children think I'm mean."

"My pastor thinks I'm very unimportant."

"They are trying to make me miserable."

How can you combat this kind of thinking? One thing you can do is check out the truth of such statements. Remember the "putting your thoughts on trial" strategy? Let's look at the first statement above, "She didn't call me because she dislikes me." Putting this thought on trial, let's first define any ambiguous terms. "Dislikes" would be a likely candidate. Let's say you define "dislikes" as "never wants to be around me." Now the statement reads "She didn't call me because she never wants to be around me." Where would you look for evidence? You might use your own experience, what others would say, and your reasoning and logic. If in the recent past this person had, in fact, spent time with you, your statement holds less water. That's using your experience to find out the truth. If others say they've heard your friend say she likes you, that would discount your mind reading even further.

For "They are trying to make me miserable," you might use reasoning and logic to put your thought on trial. Your alternate thoughts may go something like this: *What evidence do I have that others are spending many of their waking hours trying to make me miserable? Surely, they have better things to do. They do things now and then that exasperate me, but to think they are constantly and actively setting out to make me suffer seems rather farfetched.*

Magnification is one more distortion that can lead you down the path of needless anger. Recently, a discourteous motorist gave me the brights in my rear view mirror because I wasn't going fast enough for her on an icy, mountainous stretch of highway. I felt indignant that she had the nerve to be so completely unfair. I thought, *She wants me to have an accident. She's absolutely crazy* (which she may have been, since we were going down a steep incline). *I can't stand this!*

Karen and I were returning from a pleasant ski weekend, but I was quickly talking myself into a huge amount of anger and stress, all because of this little incident. Karen was my "counter" that night as she began to say, "Do you really want to get this upset over such a little thing? Let's continue to enjoy what's left of the weekend." I had to agree!

Should and *shouldn't* statements may top the list of distorted thinking that can lead to needless anger. Here are some examples:

"The world should be fair."

"People shouldn't make mistakes."

"People should always be courteous."

"If I'm nice to someone he should appreciate it."

"I should be entitled to instant gratification at all times."

"If I do something nice for her, she should reciprocate."

One good strategy for nipping *should* statements in the bud involves substituting the phrase *it would be nice if* for *should*. For example, *"It would be nice if* the world were fair. Unfortunately, as long as there is sin in the world, it will be an unfair place to live. As long as there is injustice there will be discrimination and unfairness. To say 'The world should be fair' is like saying 'The world should be perfect.' Again, *it would be nice if* the world were perfect, but in fact, it is not. Human sinfulness has taken care of that!"

It would also be nice if people were always courteous. But what a fantasy that is. Can you imagine how disillusioned you would feel if you actually bought the idea "People *should always* be courteous"? You'd feel incredulous when someone cut in front of you in traffic. You wouldn't believe it when your son didn't say "thank you" for a gift. Can you imagine how worked up you'd become daily if you believed that statement? If Christ had believed that statement, would He have tolerated the nagging crowds who tugged on His garments for healing? How would He have responded to Pilate?

And what about the statement "If I do something nice for her, she should reciprocate?" Nonsense! Everyone doesn't live by my rules, so why expect that they will? People will often treat me as kindly as I treat them, but not always.

Spineless?

I have a feeling that some of you are saying something like this: "So now, Dr. Schmidt, you're asking us to just go along with all the unfairness in the world? We're supposed to just let all injustice go by passively without any resistance? How spineless!"

No! I'm not saying that. That's going to the opposite extreme. That's complete passivity. Remember in chapter 9 we discussed the difference in aggressive, assertive, and passive behaviors? To say to yourself that things *should* be a certain way tends to lead toward aggressiveness, especially if you carry it further and repeat things such as the following to yourself: *And because people should be courteous and this guy wasn't, I'll teach him a lesson by giving him a taste of his own medicine.* Or, *I'll keep on thinking about all the nasty things I want to do to this guy until I have myself so worked up that I'll make a complete fool out of myself by fuming and yelling.* That just elevates your blood pressure. And what a neat Christian witness!

What did the Apostle James say about this? "Be . . . slow to anger, for the anger of man does not achieve the righteousness of God" (James 1:19-20). Here the Greek *orge* is being used for anger. This is the anger of revenge and it is long-lasting, like resentment. This is the type of anger that I believe unrealistic *should* statements lead to.

But if you substitute *it would be nice if* for *should,* you are more likely to react in an assertive manner. This fits in with the type of anger expressed in Ephesians 4:26. Remember, this type of anger does not involve revenge. It is not expressed in the form of a counterattack or in heated, unrestrained passion. *The mind should be in control of the emotions so that the ability to reason is not lost.*

This kind of expression of anger can lead to assertive behavior that says, in effect, to the other person, "You count and I count also." It can lead to such statements as, "When you make disparaging remarks about my parents, it makes me angry. I'd appreciate it if you'd watch yourself on that from now on."

If, instead, you were telling yourself, *My spouse* should *never criticize my parents,* your behavior would more likely be aggressive. You might be more likely to say something like, *I can't believe you can be so inconsiderate and rotten toward me. Your parents aren't so hot either* (and on and on, into a descriptive scenario of your spouse's rotten childhood).

Summary: Anger and Resentment

1. Confess your anger to God. Receive His forgiveness if you have been involved in *thumos* or *orge* types of anger.

2. Identify the probable cause of your anger. Is it frustration? Fear? Hurt? Injustice?

3. Are you expressing or tempted to express *thumos* or *orge* types of anger? Is there revenge involved? How about an explosion? Is your reason involved in the expression of your anger?

4. Identify any mental distortions you may be using. If you aren't using any distortions, perhaps your automatic thoughts are realistic and need to be expressed. If so, consider using the skills discussed in chapter 9 to confess your anger. Then it is your choice and it is between you and God as to whether expressing your anger will serve God's purposes.

5. If your thoughts involve mental distortions, challenge them, utilizing Scripture and the methods described in this chapter:

   a. List advantages and disadvantages of thinking this way.

   b. Restate your mental distortions so they are more in line with the truth.

   c. Put your thoughts on trial.

   d. Replace *should* thoughts with *it would be nice if* thoughts.

6. Choose to behave in new ways, based on your new thoughts.

12
Self-Worth: The Bottom Line

As our family crawled out of the car at our mountain cabin, nestled among some trees in the Rockies, we gazed with awe into the heavens. All around we observed a clear view of the firmament that we never see in the city. The sky was filled with stars and planets. It was almost like gazing through a powerful telescope and seeing a detailed portrait of the universe. At that moment words could not describe what we felt. David, in Psalm 8, expressed in finite words, understandable to man, what some of these feelings were:

O Lord our God, the majesty and glory of Your name fills all the earth and overflows the heavens.
. . . When I look up into the night skies and see the work of Your fingers—the moon and the stars You have made—
I cannot understand how You can bother with mere, puny man, to pay any attention to him! (Ps. 8:1, 3-4, LB)

Leslie Brandt has paraphrased this Psalm, and further captured our feelings as we contemplated the heavens:

When I gaze into star-studded skies
and attempt to comprehend the vast distances,

134

I contemplate in utter amazement
my Creator's concern for me.
I am dumbfounded that You
should care personally about me.

And yet You have made me in Your image.
You have called me Your son.
You have ordained me as Your priest
and chosen me to be Your servant.
You have assigned to me the fantastic responsibility of carrying
on Your creative activity.
O God,
how full of wonder and splendor You are!*

Let's paint a clearer picture of God's power, His concern
for us, and how we need not feel insignificant in God's sight.
We'll begin to paint this picture by taking an imaginary trip
through outer space. Let's travel at the speed of light, 186,-
000 miles per second. That's 669.6 million miles an hour!
Now that's moving rather rapidly. If I were to stand stationary
at this moment and could fire a bullet at that speed, the bullet
would dart around the earth and strike me in the back of my
head seven and one-half times faster than my normal reaction
time would allow me to move out of the way! That's fast! Let's
jump into our spaceship, then, and blast off at the speed of
light. Our destination is the backside of our own galaxy.

In about 15 minutes we've passed the sun. We figure at this
rate it will take no time, and that we'll probably be back in
time for coffee break. But then we travel for a whole day and
we still haven't reached the backside of our galaxy. We travel
2 days, 5 days, 10 days, 30 days. Still not there. We speed on
for another month, 6 months, a year, 5 years, 10 years, 20
years, 50, 100, 1,000 years. One thousand years at 669.6
million miles an hour and we still have not reached the outer
edge of our *own* galaxy! We zoom on for 5,000 years, 10,000,

---

*Leslie Brandt, *Psalms Now*. St. Louis: Concordia, 1973, p. 17.

20,000 years. We're starting to miss our families and friends!
We speed on for 30,000, 40,000, 50,000 years. Finally, traveling at the speed of light for 60,000 years we reach the outer
edge of our galaxy! Then, some wise guy in our spaceship
says, "That wasn't so bad. Let's try the next galaxy."

My friend, zipping along at this same speed of light, it
would take us a million more years to reach the *next closest*
galaxy! Would you believe that within the bowl of the Big
Dipper alone, there are a million galaxies? It's true.

Then we hear the Prophet Isaiah describing, in finite
terms, who his God is:

> "With whom will you compare Me? Who is My equal?" asks the
> Holy One. Look up into the heavens! Who created all these stars?
> As a shepherd leads his sheep, calling each by its pet name, and
> counts them to see that none are lost or strayed, so God does with
> stars and planets! (Isa. 40:25-26, LB)

And again, astronomers give us support for David's statement by indicating that they can predict the precise arrival of
the stars and planets at a given point in space within *seconds*
of their arrival and *they do arrive precisely on time*. That's
power! That's true omnipotence! Our Lord is the Shepherd of
the stars. He puts *Star Wars* to shame. He travels in seconds
among the vast distances that we traveled a moment ago for
60,000 years at the speed of light! We cannot begin to fathom
His power. Yet many have the audacity—the nerve—to
question whether God has control, whether He is Sovereign,
Leader, whether He is their Shepherd or not. Isaiah expands
on this idea:

> O Jacob, O Israel, how can you say that the Lord doesn't see your
> troubles and isn't being fair? Don't you yet understand? Don't
> you know by now that the everlasting God, the Creator of the
> farthest parts of the earth, *never* grows faint or weary? No one can
> fathom the depths of His understanding. He gives power to the
> tired and worn out, and strength to the weak. Even the youths

shall be exhausted, and the young men will all give up. But they that wait upon the Lord shall renew their strength. They shall mount up with wings like eagles; they shall run and not be weary; they shall walk and not faint (Isa. 40:27-30, LB).

Wow! What a passage. How true! If God is the Shepherd of the stars, of the vastness of the universe, if He has control over a trillion galaxies that would take humans an infinity of time and energy to explore, He would have no trouble in being *our* Shepherd. It is an insult to God to doubt whether He has enough power to help *us*. It's actually a pretty humorous question to ask, isn't it? It certainly is a relief to know that God has a sense of humor.

Again, He places Earth's people above the stars and heavens in importance. So we certainly shouldn't feel unimportant, low in self-esteem. We are worthy people; the Shepherd of the stars says so. Would you argue with the Shepherd of the stars? I'd rather argue with Darth Vader!

From this basis of being OK in God's sight we are free to move on toward perfection. Notice, I said *toward*. As Psalmist David wrote, the Lord delights in each step we take; if we fall it isn't fatal, for the Lord holds us with His hand (Ps. 37:23-24). And God's man Paul wrote, in his letter to the Christians in Philippi, "Forgetting what lies behind and reaching forward to what lies ahead, I press on toward the goal for the prize" (Phil. 3:13-14). He is saying we do not have to blame ourselves continually for missing the goal in the past, but *instead* we are to press on, keep trying, walking steadily along God's pathway.

Self-Inventory

In their *Guidebook to Dating, Waiting, and Choosing a Mate*, Norman Wright and Marvin Inmon listed several questions we should ask ourselves in working with our self-esteem. I've revised them into questions for dealing with your thought-life. Write down your own answers to the following questions:

1. How do I treat myself?

2. Have I ever thought of myself as being a parent to myself?

3. What kind of parent messages do I give myself?

4. Do I often treat myself with scorn and disrespect? If so, what are some of my "scornful" and "disrespectful" thoughts?

5. Do I sometimes punish myself? What are my self-punishing thoughts?

6. Do I expect and demand too much of myself? Again, what am I telling myself along this line?

7. Does the way I treat myself reflect on my concept of God? How would a loving God talk to me about the thoughts I've listed above?

8. Does God treat me in the same manner that I treat myself? If not, how does His treatment differ from mine?

9. What do the following Scriptures say about how I should view myself? Read them and write your responses on separate note cards.*

Psalm 139:14-16	Luke 1:37
Ephesians 2:10	Psalm 1:1
Philippians 1:6	Philippians 4:6-7
1 Peter 2:9	1 John 1:9
1 Corinthians 4:2-5	Isaiah 40:31
2 Corinthians 12:9	Psalm 32:8

When you have finished one side of a note card it might look something like this:

Side A

"Thank You for making me so wonderfully complex! It is amazing to think about. Your workmanship is marvelous—and how well I know it. You were there while I was being formed in utter seclusion! You saw me before I was born and scheduled each day of my life before I began to breathe. Every day was recorded in Your Book!"

(Psalm 139:14-16, LB)

---

*Adapted from Norman Wright, Marvin Inmon, *Guidebook to Dating, Waiting, and Choosing a Mate*. Portland, Oregon: Harvest House, 1978.

Put on the other side of the card your interpretation of what the passage says to you:

Side B
I am wonderfully made! God
made me a unique person.
He created me *exclusively* to be me.
    The Lord has been, and is
forever, *very near* me. Even
in the womb He was with me!
He keeps track of me every
second! That's incredible!

You could prepare 1 note card a day for 12 consecutive days. At the end of this time you would be armed with lots of biblical truths for warding off self-debasing thoughts. If you just carry these note cards around and read both sides at least once each day you'll be surprised at the results. God's truth regarding your worth will really begin to sink in. Remember, it is not *your* truth or *your* achievements that make you worthwhile. It is God's truth!

Performance Equals Worthiness

Does it really? Most people seem to think that performance equals worthiness. But if that's true, why did Paul write the letter to the Galatians? Often called the Magna Carta of Christian liberty, the letter to the Galatians deals with the question of whether a Gentile must become a Jew before he can become a Christian. Certain Judaizing teachers had infiltrated the churches of Galatia in central Asia Minor, which Paul had founded, declaring that in addition to having faith in Jesus Christ a Christian was obligated to keep the Mosaic Law.

Paul insisted on the contrary, that a person becomes right with God only by faith in Christ and not by his or her performance of good works.

How many people do you know who subscribe to the belief

that performance equals worthiness? Do they feel really worthy? What is the goal they set in order to achieve worthiness? Isn't their goal something like, "I will be worthwhile *if* I excel"? How many times in life does the average person excel at something? How often do you do something perfectly? I'm afraid that this kind of goal for worthiness would lead most of us to believe that we're worth just about zilch!

The tragedy of achievement is depicted in so many lives. In a movie done for television regarding a famous pop singer's life, this tragedy was graphically displayed. In one of the scenes, the singer was on the phone talking to his daughter, just before he went on stage for his first concert in Las Vegas. His daughter apparently asked him when he would be coming home. He was then separated from his wife. For a moment he began to weep bitterly, showing clearly his deep loneliness and despair. Then, as if he had slapped himself, his face became hard, poised, cool, and detached. He hurriedly and glibly said good-bye to his little girl and faced the world he was so dependent on for his worthiness.

Where was that entertainer's worth coming from? Women's screams? Millions of dollars? Fame? I can't help but think that deep down underneath it all his worthiness may have really come more from relationships. But what goal did he act on? Where did he *think* his worth came from?

The Sensation of Being Somebody

Dr. Maurice Wagner suggests that there are three sources of self-esteem: competence, belongingness, and worthiness.*

Competence relates to achievements. It is a feeling of adequacy. It is built on one's accomplishments, past and present.

Belongingness is the awareness of being accepted, wanted, and cared for. It is a sense of being a significant part of a group of people. There is the sense that you will be missed if absent from the group.

---

*Maurice Wagner, *The Sensation of Being Somebody*, Grand Rapids: Zondervan, 1975.

Worthiness is the feeling, "I am OK," "I count," and "I am all right." It is a feeling that we are accepted by others. Worthiness involves sharing who we are and what we believe and being accepted with our good points and bad points.

So often we get stuck in the *competence* circle only. Then we tell ourselves such things as:

I will be worthwhile if I do that thing well.

Making mistakes is terrible.

I expect myself to excel. If I don't I'm not worthwhile.

Wagner is not saying that competence is an illegitimate source of self-esteem. But he *is* saying that if we focus only on the competence area, excluding belongingness and worthiness, we're in real trouble. Why? Because without a sense that we can be accepted for *who* we are as well as what we do, we serve under the tyranny of *earning* our worth, and even our salvation.

Thank God that many men today are understanding more completely the value of friendships, belonging to a group, and intimacy. No longer is the model of manhood so clearly found in the macho man, a Clint Eastwood or a John Wayne who rides off into the sunset alone.

Self-Worth: an Illusion

"What do you mean an illusion? You, a psychologist suggesting that self-worth is an illusion? Now you've really lost your grip! You don't quite have all your oars in the water, Dr. Schmidt!" Am I reading your thoughts correctly? How can I suggest that self-worth is an illusion? Well, for one, Paul continually suggested that following the letter of Jewish laws did not a Christian make. Jesus constantly underlined this point as well. And besides, what is *self*-worth anyway? If you make more money than I do, does *that* make you a better person? Or are you better than I if you hold a more prestigious position? Or a less prestigious position? Or what about if you give more to the poor? Perhaps you are better than I am if you are a preacher, or a brain surgeon, or a senator? Maybe I'm better than *you* because I'm an author, or because I can catch more trout in a stream?

Do you see it? How in the world does anyone decide on *who* is more worthwhile or what makes up self-worth? Certainly we can make specific comparisons. We can make judgments, for example, that one football player is better than another. Or that one musician is more talented than another, etc. But we can't always agree on that, can we? Wouldn't it be even more absurd to say that a certain person is more full of self-worth than another? We don't even know for sure what self-worth is.

Paul told the Romans and us, "Just as there are many parts to our bodies, so it is with Christ's body. We are all parts of it, and it takes every one of us to make it complete, for we each have different work to do. So we belong to each other, and each needs all the others" (Rom. 12:4-5, LB). Here is more proof that the idea of *one* person having more *self*-worth than another is missing the point and is probably not a helpful concept at all.

So what's the bottom line? It's what God has done for us. That's the bottom line. Dr. Lloyd Ahlem, in *Do I Have to Be Me?*, summarizes my own thoughts here so well:

"The writers of the Scriptures are careful to point out that when God looks at you in Jesus Christ, He sees you as a brother of His own Son. Because of the work of Christ, all the ugliness of humanity is set aside. You are worth all of God's attention. If you were the only person in the whole world, it would be worth God's effort to make Himself known to you. He gives you freely the status and adequacy of an heir to the universe.

"This is *agape* love, the unmerited, unconditional favor of God for man. *We achieve our adequacy through this unceasing love.* We do not *become* sufficient, approved, or adequate; rather we are *declared to be* such! When we believe this, we become achievers and humanitarians as an effect, a by-product of our newfound selves. . . . When a person has accepted adequacy as a gift, he immediately perceives a new standard for achievement. No longer does the contention of human

Victor Books to Improve the Inner You

Gaining Through Losing—Evelyn Christenson
God can take the disappointments and tragedies in your life and turn them into unbelievable gains. (6-2344)

Healing for Damaged Emotions—David A. Seamands
Satan uses many emotional problems to keep you from reaching spiritual maturity. Learn how to heal these problems with God's help. (6-2228)

The Power of a Positive Self-Image—Clifford Baird
You can achieve your full success potential as you develop a strong and healthy self-image. (6-2316)

Transformed by Thorns—Grant Martin
Stress, anger, worry, and depression are just a few of life's thorns. Discover how your problems and hurts can transform you spiritually. (6-2397)

performance apply, but rather the measure of faithfulness judges us. This is the fair standard, the one that stimulates everyone, frustrates no one, and is administered by the providential will of God."*

And how do we learn about this fair standard? We learn about it in Scripture. We are to "let this mind be in [us,] which was also in Christ Jesus" (Phil. 2:5, KJV). You see, if we think like Christ we will act more and more like Him. But thinking like Him means getting rid of the foolish "tapes" that we presently play in our minds, and replacing them with "Jesus tapes."

---

*Lloyd Ahlem, *Do I Have to Be Me?* Ventura, Calif: Regal Books, 1973, pp. 1, 73.